BRITISH MUSEUM PATTERN BOOKS

Roman Designs

BRITISH MUSEUM PATTERN BOOKS

Roman Designs

EVA WILSON

BRITISH MUSEUM ⬛ PRESS

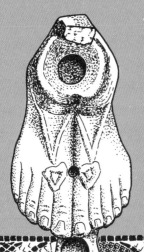

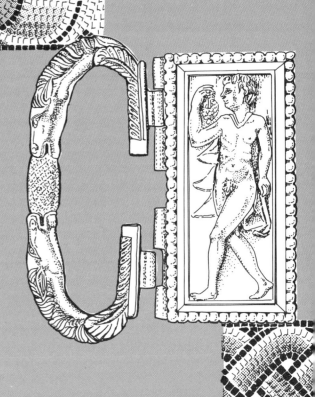

© 1999 Eva Wilson

Published by
British Museum Press
A division of The British
Museum Company Ltd
46 Bloomsbury Street, London
WC1B 3QQ

First published 1999

British Library Cataloguing in
Publication Data
A catalogue record for this
book is available from the
British Library

ISBN 0–7141–8078–5

Designed by Roger Davies

Typeset in Palatino by
Wyvern 21
Printed in Great Britain by
Page Bros, Norwich

Acknowledgements
I am most grateful to the staff
of the British Museum for
their support during the
preparation of the drawings
in this book. I am particularly
grateful to Catherine Johns for
her patience and advice. I
thank Jack Ogden for
permission to publish the
drawing which appears at the
bottom of **89**. I am very much
indebted to Roger Rawcliffe,
who taught me what little I
know of Roman history and
looked with indulgence on
my manuscript in draft. His
enthusiasm for the enterprise
and his advice have been
invaluable.

Contents

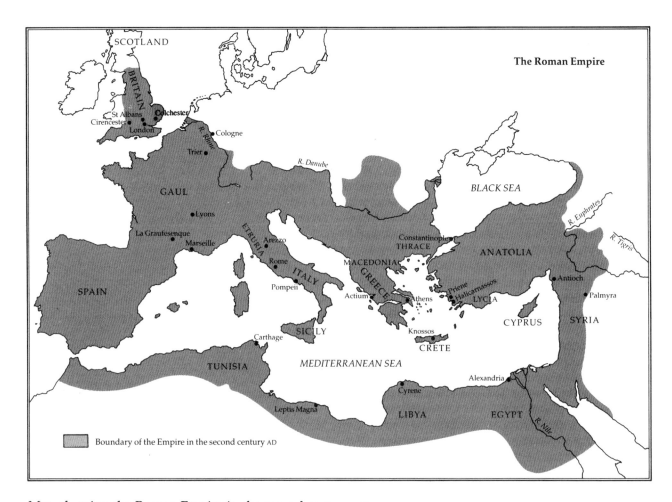

Map showing the Roman Empire in the second century AD.

Introduction

The achievement of the Romans in the field of decorative art must not be underestimated; indeed we have the Romans to thank for nearly every common motif used in Western decorative and applied art today. Their motifs were those which had long been current in the Mediterranean, most recently in Hellenistic art. In the extensive lands conquered by Alexander the Great (d. 323 BC) – who had extended Greek culture beyond Greece itself to Cyprus, Asia Minor, the Middle East and Egypt – and in those states created by his successors, this heritage was transformed into a sophisticated cosmopolitan, learned and art-loving culture of high material standard. The Romans developed more robust and practical forms of these ancient motifs, suitable for the mass production which became necessary to meet their seemingly insatiable demands for decoration. It was in these forms that classical Mediterranean motifs were distributed throughout the provinces of the Empire from the eastern Mediterranean to Britain, where they greatly influenced art and ornament long after the Romans had departed. Here I outline the origins and use of some of the major motifs – lotus, palmette, acanthus, leaf scrolls, the hunt, geometric interlace and others. I shall also consider some aspects of the crafts and techniques which developed in the Roman world to serve the more robust style and mass production of pottery, metalwork and mosaics. These techniques are in most cases still in use today.

Around 500 BC Rome was a small republic on the River Tiber in Latium (Lazio) in central Italy, one of many Latin city-states. Immediately to the north were the Etruscans, the dominant power in the area and a people of different racial origin, speaking a different language; along the southern coasts were cities occupied by descendants of Greek colonists. In other parts of Italy to the south and east lived Italic peoples such as the Sabines and the Samnites. The result was a rich mixture of Greek and Etruscan cultural influences together with strong elements of indigenous Italic culture. Thus, for example, the Romans initially used Etruscan burial customs and temple plans. Temples and other buildings were of wood and the roof structure was protected by plaques of moulded and painted fired clay (terracotta) which covered exposed timber. These roofs had openwork crests which, like the plaques, were moulded in sections, fitted together and painted, most commonly in white or cream, red and black (2–9). New plaques could be moulded to the old patterns and added as repairs became necessary. Designs could therefore be repeated over long periods. While in the Greek world stone began to replace wood in temples by the second half of the seventh century, in Italy, where no local supply of suitable building-stone was recognised at the time, the use of wood and terracotta continued for several centuries more.

Rome increasingly dominated the other city-states, which became subservient in a relationship more often based on mutual interest and enforced loyalty than outright conquest. By the third century BC Rome's allies extended over much of Italy, and Rome's power was increasingly recognised by the Hellenistic world in Macedonia across the Adriatic, by the Ptolemies in Egypt and throughout the eastern Mediterranean. At this time Rome began a campaign (the Punic Wars) against the Carthaginians, who controlled most of the western Mediterranean seaboard. The Carthaginians were originally Phoenicians from Syria, an ancient mercantile nation with trading posts all round the Mediterranean. Carthage, on the north coast of Tunisia, had been founded in the ninth or eighth century BC and had become an independent state of great power and wealth. The three major wars it fought with Rome, however, gradually drained its resources – by 201 BC Carthage had lost its overseas provinces to Rome, and in 146 BC it was finally destroyed.

The victories of Republican Rome were celebrated by triumphant parades of prisoners and loot, which could include art treasures as well as weapons and other spoils of war. Among the rich booty from the sacking of the great Greek city of Syracuse in Sicily in 211 BC, for example, were objects decorated with art reflecting the conquered people's ancient history and culture. Artists and architects were brought to Rome to create buildings in which the booty could be displayed. High-status objects of monumental and other prestigious art were looted to furnish the emerging capital of Rome. Italian marble was now available from quarries in the Apuan Alps in Tuscany (Carrara), and temples were built in this material in the styles and construction techniques of the established Greek Orders, particularly in the Corinthian version of the Ionic Order (10–13). For other public and private buildings another type of construction developed which used brick and lime mortar concrete. The Romans did not invent the arch or the barrel vault, but their outstanding contribution to architectural history was the practical application of these two elements, using them together with the newly invented lime mortar concrete which could stand up on its own and carry great weight. Walls were, however, normally faced with stone, plaster or brick and the facing would feature elements of classical temple architecture purely as decoration.

In the course of the second century BC booty came from Greece itself in the wake of repeated campaigns against Alexander the Great's successors in the eastern Mediterranean. Triumphant parades in Rome now displayed statuary as well as art of all kinds – paintings, furniture, textiles – all in a Hellenistic style which represented unheard-of luxury in Rome. Statuary and monuments from classical Greece (i.e., from the fifth and fourth centuries BC) were also included and – once re-erected – were dedicated to Roman gods. The Romans of the Republic, with their ideals of austerity, had ambivalent attitudes to the highly sophisticated mainly Greek or Hellenistic art of their supposedly decadent but culturally superior vanquished subjects. In time, however, the military commanders grew accustomed to this wealth and kept some of the riches for themselves. With the booty came artists, architects and scholars – most of the artists in the Roman world were Greeks or from Asia Minor or the Near East, where they had been trained in the Hellenistic artistic tradition. The genius of Rome, however, found its expression in harnessing the skills of these artists to different purposes, while at the same time remaining aware of their superior artistic sensibilities. In the words of the Roman poet Virgil, writing in the first century BC, *Exudent alii spirantia mollius aera . . . vivos decent de marmore vultus* (Others will beat out the breathing bronze more softly . . . and will draw living faces from marble) (*Aeneid*, VI 847–8).

The last great triumphant parade in the Republican manner followed the defeat of Antony and Cleopatra at the Battle of Actium in 31 BC. The victor of the battle, Octavian (63 BC–14 AD), received the name of Augustus in 27 BC and transformed the Republic into an Empire. To the north and east the boundaries of this Empire could now be defined by the rivers Rhine and Danube, while to the south it encompassed the entire Mediterranean together with the surrounding countries as far west as the Atlantic and as far east as the Black Sea and the Euphrates. By the time of the death of Augustus the growth of the Empire had nearly come to an end and the conquest of Britain, begun in AD 47 under Claudius (ruled AD 41–54), was the only lasting addition. The early years of the Empire were a period of expanding markets, increased investment in industry and the rapid exploitation of new territories. A massive demand from the army and the provinces transformed traditional Greek skills in pottery, glass, metalwork and other crafts into thriving industries which distributed their products to all areas of the Empire as part of the huge cargoes of staples such as corn, oil and wine.

Augustus moderated his Republican predecessors' custom of victory parades, and loot was placed instead on public display. The Romans of the Empire learnt to love opulence and wanted everything to be appropriately decorated. There was a great demand for monumental sculpture and other ornament to fulfil the desire for the suitable decoration and fitting out of public buildings and public places. Throughout the Empire, a concept known as *decor* (meaning the selection of a style suited to its setting) was applied equally to private houses and to domestic arrangements. Walls were painted, floors covered with mosaic panels, cups and plates decorated in approved styles. The rich and powerful wore fashionable jewellery in precious metals and stones.

Augustus used his power as emperor to define an art style based on classical Greek models which was used to embellish the city and court. His great monument the *Ara Pacis Augustae* (Altar of Augustan Peace) introduced an acanthus scroll which, while seeking to emulate the art of classical Greece, was a version of this well-known motif far more elaborate and rich in detail than anything the Greeks had achieved (**14–15**).

During the period of the emperor Hadrian (ruled AD 117–38) there was a less restrained and more broadly based revival of the taste for classical Greek style. Motifs originally intended only for public monuments were adopted for private use, as can be seen in the decoration of private houses where the acanthus scroll used on the *Ara Pacis Augustae*, for example, became popular in many media. Even the imperial eagle and the personification of Victory were used in domestic settings (**16, 60**).

A long period of peaceful consolidation came to an end in the third century. The late Roman Empire was always on the defensive against pressure from beyond the frontiers: the Empire itself was then divided and in AD 330 Constantine established a Christian city at Byzantium as a new capital in the east. (The decorative art of the Byzantine Empire, which survived until the capture of Constantinople by the Turks in 1453, is not included in this book.) The western Empire suffered defeats by Germanic tribes who gradually overran its provinces in Europe and North Africa. Alaric, king of the Visigoths, invaded Italy and sacked Rome in AD 410. The last emperor of the western Roman Empire was deposed in AD 476.

Britain became a province of the Roman Empire in AD 43 and Roman rule ended formally about AD 410. For nearly 400 years, therefore, Latin was the official language in Britain, the laws, administration and currency were those of Rome, and the religions and art of the Mediterranean predominated. The beliefs and tastes of the Celtic society were not, however, entirely replaced, for a distinctive Romano-British culture gradually emerged over many generations and is reflected in the arts, where Celtic motifs can be identified in decoration and where Celtic gods can perhaps be identified in the Roman pantheon (**45, 92**). Nor did this culture come to a halt at the end of Roman rule. Lowland Britain was gradually settled by a mixture of Germanic tribes from north-western Germany and Denmark, and the flowing spirals of Celtic ornament, along with the orderly framework and animal motifs of the Roman decorative tradition, together contributed to create the exceptionally successful art of the Anglo-Saxons.

Decorative motifs in the Roman world

The great majority of the motifs used in Roman decoration are of Mediterranean origin. Motifs created in the ancient Near East became central to the development of art further to the east, as well as in the Mediterranean and in Europe generally. The eastern Mediterranean seaboard and its hinterland formed the crossroads of the most important trade routes of the ancient world and served as a clearing house for ideas of all kinds. With trade, knowledge of patterns and designs was disseminated by a variety of means: as high-status gifts between rulers in the cause of political power games; through the actual goods traded; by means of seals, painted containers and patterned cloth which accompanied humbler trade goods, and in many other related ways. Let us now turn to a consideration of the major motif groups which resulted from all this political and trading activity.

Lotus and palmette (2–13)

The lotus motif developed before the Roman period in Egypt and, while clearly based on water lilies, had already found its highly conventionalised form in the third millennium BC as the triangular outline of an open flower-head with an arrangement of thin petals between three calyx leaves. The design often includes a bud on either side of the flower (4).

Trade and exchange of ideas took place continually between Egypt, the ancient Near East and the Aegean, particularly during the period of the eighteenth dynasty (c.1550–1307 BC). The lotus motif, together with other floral motifs in Egyptian art – the papyrus, the palm and the lily – became widely used in western Asia, where the dominant motif was the spiral. From these elements the palmette motif gradually emerged as the distillation of the most successful features of several motifs, notably the symmetrical spiral base and the fan-shaped uprights (6). The two motifs – lotus and palmette – came together in borders, where they alternate in the same manner as in the lotus-and-bud border designs mentioned above (4–5, 12 ABOVE).

In the sixth century BC, at a time of expansion when Greek colonies were being widely established around the Mediterranean, lotus and palmette designs on exported painted pottery spread the knowledge of these motifs to other areas. Temple decorations of terracotta in west central Italy, where the motifs are used with many variations, have already been mentioned (2–9).

The Doric, Ionic and Corinthian Orders (10–13)

The Orders of classical architecture were formalised by the Greeks and applied to the design and proportions of buildings using the post-and-lintel, or column and entablature, construction. The Doric Order emerged in the sixth century BC, and was followed by the Ionic Order in the east Greek territories of Anatolia. The mouldings of the entablature of the Ionic Order – that is the architrave, frieze and cornice – include the egg-and-dart, leaf-and-dart and waterleaf, all of which are broadly based on lotus-and-bud and palmette motifs (11). Other decorative borders such as the bead-and-reel and astragal (11) look convincingly as if they were originally turned in wood, for architectural decoration in wood preceded what was later carried out in stone.

The Doric Order of architecture was little used by the Romans in Italy. The Tuscan Order was a simplified version with base, unfluted shaft and simply moulded capital. The Ionic Order, however, became popular and its enrichments were further elaborated (10–12).

The Corinthian Order (which is more properly regarded as a variation of the Ionic) was mainly used in the interiors of Greek temples in the fourth century BC. It became dominant in Roman architecture in response to a taste for more decorative styles and for its easier adaptation to different features, such as engaged columns and pilasters (13). The Corinthian capital made use of the acanthus leaf as its major motif, like the purely Roman variation, the Composite capital, which has horizontally linked volutes of Ionic type set over a bell of acanthus leaves.

Acanthus (12–19)

Leaf borders and scroll motifs were used extensively in the art and architecture of ancient Greece and Rome. Foremost of these was the acanthus motif. Large and small acanthus leaves were added to scrolls and palmettes to make these abstract motifs more plant-like. Leaves added at the bases of the lotus and palmette elements produced designs now usually known as *anthemion* or honeysuckle (12). (There is no reason to believe that there was a conscious attempt to portray this flower; the name is used in the sense of being honeysuckle-like.)

The ornamental leaf motif known as acanthus has long been associated with the plant of that name (14). In the capital of the Corinthian Order, the spirals which support the abacus at the top – the volutes – spring from a double row of acanthus leaves. The Roman architect Vitruvius wrote in the first century BC about the origins of the Corinthian capital (13). He tells the story of the sculptor Kallimachos who, seeing curving acanthus leaves growing around a basket of toys left on the tomb of a small girl, became inspired to create the first Corinthian capital. The story, although clearly an invention, is interesting in that it shows the early connection between this ornamental leaf motif and the plant.

The acanthus scroll which decorates panels on the monumental altar the *Ara Pacis Augustae*, of which a small detail is illustrated here (15), demonstrates a mixture of realistic plant elements, like the ribbed stalk and curling leaf, together with flowers and tendrils from real or imaginary plants and half-palmettes. This particular acanthus scroll, far richer in detail than anything produced in classical Greece, has been regarded as an ideal of Greek-inspired ornament whenever classical Greek art has been admired and emulated. While close to home in Italy the acanthus motif retained a fairly realistic form, elsewhere, in eastern parts of the Empire, where Hellenistic tastes prevailed, the motif became more elegant and floral. In Roman Carthage acanthus scrolls on mosaics form thickets of abundant stylised foliage, while in Britain the acanthus motif became a very restrained and formalised leaf scroll (18–19). Throughout most of its long history the leaf ornament generally known as acanthus is in fact an imaginary leaf adapted to many uses.

Laurel, olive, ivy, vine scrolls and garlands (20–27)

While no symbolism attaches to the acanthus motif, other decorative motifs based on plants were associated with religious beliefs and ritual. Throughout the Mediterranean area, including the Near and Middle East, cults shared many traits. These were concerned with natural phenomena and powers – an underworld to be feared, the sun, moon and stars, trees, the sea and, of course, love and fertility in all their many aspects – which had to be cultivated, worshipped and appeased. Such powers and phenomena were personified as gods and goddesses who were recognised by specific attributes (24, 60, 66, 74, 76, 86). In the Greek and Roman pantheon and mythology these attributes were often plants, while wreaths of leaves and flowers were also used as marks of distinction, being worn by victors of wars or public games and as emblems of office. The wreath used many motifs based on leaves, flowers and fruit. Among the most frequently used leaf borders are those based on laurel, olive, ivy and vine, all in more or less conventionalised forms. While laurel is associated with victory, ivy and vine are both associated with Bacchus. They are common motifs in vase painting and decorate many cups and vessels used at the table as well as being present in representations of the popular Bacchic cult which involved copious wine drinking. Another motif used in this context is the cantharus, a wine cup with two handles (45–48).

Garlands of plants and fruit suspended between the horned skulls of rams, oxen or bulls decorate altars, funerary monuments and temples, reflecting the significance and popularity of animal sacrifice (22).

Spiral, meander, key pattern and the maze (28–30)

The spiral is a universal element in all decoration, in primitive as well as in the most sophisticated art. The running spiral (also known as running dog, wave scroll or Vitruvian scroll) and the meander (also known as Greek fret, Greek key, labyrinth, maze, key pattern) are curved and angular variations of the same motif. Other figures, for example the four-strand spiral and the swastika, are similarly related.

Spiral and meander motifs, and their intermediate forms, have a long history in the Mediterranean. They occur in the earliest farming communities in Anatolia in the sixth millennium BC and as major motifs in pottery decoration throughout neolithic Europe. In the third millennium BC spirals decorated stone monuments in western Europe, in the Iberian peninsula and on Malta. Later, during the second millennium BC, spirals and scrolls were the basic form from which the Minoan potters created a new art in the Mediterranean. Designs based on spirals, scrolls, concentric circles and meandering bands are typical of the art of the Mycenaean civilisation on the Greek mainland in the middle of the second millennium BC. Meanders and key patterns are today closely associated with Greek art and architecture. In the formalised Orders of architecture the meander motif was assigned to flat vertical surfaces. In the eighteenth-century European revival of interest in classical Greece as a source of ornament, it was the meander and key patterns which, above all others, signified Greek style and taste.

It is generally accepted that the name of the motif refers to the winding river Meander in Anatolia, Turkey. This appears to be an ancient connection, since coins of the late fourth century BC from the towns on this river feature the meander motif (30 ABOVE LEFT, TOP). The connection with water perhaps persists in Roman times, when the motif is frequently used on mosaic floors in bath houses. With few exceptions, these motifs carry no symbolic messages in Greek and Roman art.

In Greek vase painting of the fifth century BC, however, the meander became associated with a popular story drawn from the legends concerning King Minos of Crete, the story of Theseus slaying the Minotaur and finding his way in and out of the Labyrinth. In these representations Theseus and the Minotaur – part bull, part man – are shown as realistic figures, while the Labyrinth is often indicated by a simple meander border, attached to a door post or pillar representing the entrance (30 ABOVE RIGHT). In these scenes, therefore, the meander border became the conventional sign or ideogram for the Labyrinth. When the cities of Crete began to issue coins, the link between this story and the island of Crete was so strong that the motifs chosen to represent Knossos, the Minotaur and the Labyrinth were taken from its legendary history relating to a period some thousand years earlier. At first the Labyrinth took the form of a meander; later, in the fourth century BC, the form of the Labyrinth was that of a 'true' maze, a design which can be traced back at least to the second millennium BC in the Mediterranean (30 ABOVE LEFT). Apparently in an unbroken tradition, the true maze occurs in the east from the Caucasus to Java, as it does in Europe, to the present day.

Maze designs in mosaic pavements have a wide distribution in the western provinces of the Roman Empire. The design illustrated 30 is from Pompeii, but the same four-fold version of the true maze design occurs elsewhere. A number of examples are known, for instance, from Britain. Several reasons for their popularity, other than their obvious decorative quality, have been suggested, among them the hope that 'on rainy days they would provide a source of quiet amusement for children'!

Intersecting circles, geometric constructions and perspective (31–47)

In Roman public and private building many decorative motifs were based on geometrical constructions which shared the disciplines of proportion and size with the structures they embellished. Decorative designs based on geometrical figures are basically simple: they can be constructed easily with only a compass and a rule and by the application of certain procedures which produce triangles, squares, hexagons and stars. Such designs can be reduced and enlarged with great ease. Geometrical constructions were exploited to the full in the designs of Roman mosaic pavements (40–46).

Intersecting circles are the basis for a large number of designs, from stars and rosettes to twists and plaits and area-filling patterns of many kinds (31–34, 72). Sometimes they are the necessary underlying grids on which designs are drawn, while in other examples the use of colour brings out different patterns from the same constructions. The decorative potential of intersecting circles was known in the ancient world and was enthusiastically exploited by Roman craftsmen.

The twist and the plait were among several motifs of western Asian origin which provided the inspiration for enrichments in the established Orders of Greek architecture. In Roman decoration they serve as common elements, borders and framework constructions (39, 41–44). They are decorative conventionalised motifs and have, with few exceptions, no symbolic meaning. They do not, as a rule, appear to portray real plaits in a functional capacity.

Twists, plaits and interlacing designs produce a sense of three-dimensional effect by the impression that one strand passes over and under another, a feature sometimes reinforced by shading (39). Other decorative motifs and representations of architectural enrichments in particular are also shaded in this manner (29 BELOW, 35). This treatment is sometimes erroneously called an isometric projection or perspective. Wall paintings often show scenes of rooms and buildings which also appear to be drawn in perspective. It would appear, however, that while three-dimensional representations do occur in Greece (used in particular for scene painting as described by contemporary writers), this was based more on observation than on an understanding of the theories behind the phenomenon of lines receding to a point. Similarly, while the Roman artist often achieved striking effects with illusions of this kind – indeed many mosaic floor designs are most cunning optical illusions – the effects were based on observation and experience, not theoretical calculations. The three-dimensional effects and optical illusions were clearly much enjoyed and used by the Romans, often with dizzying effect (34–35, 40–41, 100), but the understanding of true perspective and its application in art, with a vanishing point common to all the features of a scene, was achieved only during the Renaissance.

Knots, however, by virtue of the obvious symbolism of joining and uniting as well as by their practical uses in everyday life, are universal motifs in art and have a multitude of realistic as well as symbolic applications. The reef knot is sometimes known as 'Knot of Herakles' (Hercules). This relates to the knot with which Herakles tied the skin of the Nemean lion around his shoulders by its legs, which appears on many representations of this popular story. The reef knot motif became the fashion on jewellery from the time of Alexander the Great, who liked to compare himself to the heroic Herakles (87). In more recent times knot motifs in jewellery were given as love tokens, as they still are today. The so-called 'Solomon's knot' – the origin of whose name is obscure and which is not in fact a true knot at all – is a very popular motif especially in mosaic designs (38).

Figures, animals, composite and imaginary creatures (50–76)

Many common animal motifs first encountered on seals dating from the fifth to the first millennia BC in the ancient Near East have remained in fashion for thousands of years. Scenes of combat between hunter and hunted and fantastic creatures made up of different animal parts are prominent among them. Scenes are arranged in symmetrical compositions of opposed figures, while depictions of the human form usually represent gods, goddesses and other superhuman beings (50).

The Greek repertoire of scenes and motifs with their decorative attributes was taken over by the Romans, in whose art and mythology they were sometimes adapted to a different story. Among the gods, Neptune and Oceanus with their attributes of dolphins and other sea creatures were popular in decoration (54–56, 66–71), as were the many associations with Bacchus and his cult of wine drinking and feasting (24–25, 48, 74). It is not always possible, however, to distinguish between cult figures and decoration. A cult figure may be reserved for very specific uses and be regarded with awe, but the same figure or motif in another context can be used simply as a pleasing design, with the additional advantage of being regarded as a good omen or as a sign to ward off evil in an atmosphere of vague superstition.

Some of these creatures were composites (i.e. figures which combine attributes of two or more species), which were incorporated into mythology and legend and given names and characters. One of these occurs in a story which has already been mentioned: that of the hero Theseus, who killed the Cretan Minotaur, a creature often represented as a man with a bull's head (30). Another hero, Bellerophon, killed a composite creature, the 'chimera', a fire-breathing, lion-headed creature with a goat's head emerging from its back and the tail of a snake (50–51).

The twelve signs of the zodiac are among the most important of the conventionalised and sometimes composite animal forms. Based on astronomical observations first carried out in Mesopotamia, the zodiac, in the modern astrological sense, was defined in the fourth century BC when a catalogue of the stars was drawn up by Greek astronomers and the name 'zodiac' first used. Since many of the animals of the zodiac are in any case popular motifs – lion, bull and fish, for example – it is not always possible to establish in individual cases whether a design is a reference to a zodiac sign. On a roof finial, for example, the winged figure of Victory is shown standing on a globe and bearing a captured trophy of weapons and armour. On either side are creatures with goats' heads and fish tails (60). The association with the ever victorious emperor Augustus makes the attribution to the zodiac sign of Capricorn likely in this case, as this was his birth sign.

When Christianity became the sole official religion of the Roman Empire in AD 380 it had already co-existed for a period with other beliefs. Throughout most of the fourth century artists were working for patrons of many faiths, and the existing conventions were used to illustrate Christian as well as non-Christian themes. Christian symbols such as, for example, the creatures described in Revelation and those later assigned to the four Apostles, therefore took the familiar contemporary forms of the eagle, lion, bull and man and were at times treated as composite creatures by the addition of wings. In representations of the story of Bellerophon, the chimera can be seen to be modelled on similar fantastic animals of ancient Near Eastern tradition (50–51). Such compositions became the basis in Christian art for representations of St George and the Dragon, St Michael or other similar examples of good fighting evil.

The hunt was a very popular form of the combat motif; it celebrates an activity, more a pastime than a matter of life and death, which can be given a romantic or heroic interpretation and which only occasionally needs to be regarded as symbolic. Hunting was a major preoccupation of all – a favoured leisure activity of the mighty as well as of the common man – and the hunt is a common motif in Roman decoration, on mosaics, silver and domestic pottery (52–53, 83). Long after the collapse of the Roman Empire, many of these motifs survived as part of the common stock of European decorative art. While the popularity of hunting as a pastime and sport may account for its widespread use as a decorative motif in medieval Europe, a link with its Roman past can be identified in the more exotic animals which often occur in hunting scenes far from their natural habitat. Sometimes a scene may reveal a huntsman's close observation of his prey. The animals on the frieze on a bowl in the Traprain Treasure are drawn in such detail that particular species of animals have been identified (52), in an assemblage which suggests that the bowl may have been made in the eastern Mediterranean, the Middle East or Egypt, where this group of animals occurs together.

Natural representation is sometimes touchingly evident in Roman art. A fondness for dogs is evident in a head delicately modelled in bronze as a lamp (65) and in the 'guard dogs' portrayed in mosaic on the floors of Pompeii (100). At Chedworth the conventional representations of the seasons on the floor of the dining room show a delightfully lightly clad girl as 'Spring', while 'Winter' portrays a frozen Roman wrapped up warmly for that season in Gloucestershire (57).

Not all representations are so naturalistic. A classical idealised traditional style is often beautiful and elegant (17, 45, 49, 54, 68, 74, 76), but there is also a stronger, almost grotesque, though equally formalised, face (55, 58, 62, 63, 66).

Because this book does not deal with statues and portrait sculpture this important aspect of Roman art is not represented here. In minor ways, smaller figures for domestic use and representations in silver, bronze and pottery can reveal a high quality of modelling and interpretation (61–62, 64–65, 71, 83, 97). A scene from the chariot races in the Circus Maximus in Rome on a clay lamp (96) is a skilful evocation of a complicated scene, leaving the viewer with a lively impression of speed in a crowded place.

Colour

The Romans, like the Greeks before them, painted marble statuary and architectural detail in strong decorative or naturalistic colours with details sometimes picked out in gold. The use of highly coloured decorative stones like, for example, the red *rosso antico* marble from southern Greece and the purple porphyry from Egypt confirms a taste for colour. The effect under the bright Mediterranean sun would have been brilliant – but to our eyes probably vulgar and garish. It was after it was stripped of its colours to reveal the subtle elegance of plain white marble that the art of classical Greece and Rome left its enduring legacy in European art and architecture in the neo-classical style and formed our own taste. For a more realistic view it is important, therefore, to think of the private and public buildings of the Romans as a riot of colour; to think of opulence rather than restraint. The Romans used lavish decoration in their houses, and the motifs described above were applied very freely to walls and floors as well as to objects in everyday use.

Roman decoration and crafts

Methods of building, manufacture and craftwork in the Roman world drew on the traditional skills of the craftsmen who came to Rome from all parts of the Empire. The eruption of Vesuvius in AD 79 buried the cities of Pompeii and Herculaneum, allowing us to learn a good deal about the houses, furnishings and objects in daily use. Buildings elsewhere, though less well preserved, also provide much information about daily life. Archaeological excavations uncover workshops and tools, which provide clues about how things were made. The objects themselves, however – the pots, lamps and silver dishes (particularly where they are broken or unfinished) – are sometimes even more informative. Contemporary writers also contribute to our knowledge of the materials and techniques used.

The history of Pompeii and Herculaneum had stretched back several centuries before the sudden disaster of AD 79. The towns were Greek colonial cities, the houses of Greek type with rooms grouped round a central hall, colonnaded courtyards and gardens – a domestic architecture suited to a hot climate. The houses of the rich were built and decorated to a high standard with frescoes, mosaics, statuary and well-designed gardens. Similar high standards are found elsewhere in Italy as well as in the provinces. Freestone, stone rubble and brick were used, together with lime mortar and plaster. The use of lime mortar was an important Roman innovation, in that it allowed all this building activity to take place at great speed and to be of high quality.

Walls decorated with painting were common in the ancient Mediterranean world before Roman times, and the techniques used by Roman painters were based on the methods used by craftsmen of earlier periods. The excellent quality of the stucco developed by the Romans, however, allowed techniques to be refined to a very high level of craftsmanship.

Wall paintings on stucco were praised by contemporary writers and favourably compared to the work of famous painters in other media of the period, of which little or nothing is preserved. It is therefore reasonable to suppose that wall painters were the leaders of fashion among applied artists. Wall paintings at Pompeii and Herculaneum demonstrate changes in fashion over time. Four distinctive styles of painting were identified by the Roman architect Vitruvius. In the first, walls are painted to imitate marble facing, while in the second and third styles architectural compositions in dark colours give the illusion of perspective on several planes. Figures of mythological, heroic or cult subjects were introduced, and in the fourth style, in the period before the catastrophe of AD 79, fantastic landscapes, architecture and furniture are painted against light backgrounds with masks and mythological themes.

The walls of vaults built in country houses over natural or artificial springs were decorated to look like natural grottoes with pumice stones and shells set in rustic mosaic. Pieces of brightly coloured glass were gradually introduced into these elaborate decorations alongside the natural materials. In Rome and central Italy mosaics of this type became popular during the second and third centuries AD; later the same skills and techniques were employed in the early Christian mosaics in Rome and Ravenna. Floor mosaics were produced by a different set of craftsmen and followed different traditions.

Mosaic floors and pavements (34–47)

Floor mosaics of natural pebbles are known throughout the ancient Mediterranean world. Mosaic pavements with borders, and sometimes incorporating a colourful centrepiece, developed in the Hellenistic world and were well established before 100 BC. Skilful mosaicists used very small stones to imitate painting. In the Roman period the Hellenistic techniques and motifs, although adapted to changed circumstances, were passed on.

In Republican and early Imperial Italy floors and pavements were simply made of concrete, some embellished with a few stones set in a pattern. Other floors were laid in geometric patterns with stones and marbles of different colours cut to simple shapes; these could have considerable impact when laid to produce optical illusions (34).

Mosaic floors proper were made from small pieces, usually cubes, cut from a variety of materials such as coloured stone, clay tiles, pottery or glass (recycled material from building sites could be used). The individual elements in a pavement are known collectively as *tesserae*.

There were several ways of laying this kind of mosaic. The individual tesserae could be set directly into the bedding mortar. Alternatively, a section of the design would first be set in sand, and paper or cloth would be glued to the upper surface; the resulting panel would then be lifted and set in place in soft mortar; finally, when this was dry the glue would be dissolved in water and the cover removed. In a third option the tesserae were glued face down on a coloured cartoon of paper or cloth showing the design. When the section was turned over and set in place the cartoon was removed, the design appearing in reverse.

The overall layout of the design would have to consider the shape and size of the space to be covered. A geometrically based framework or grid which could be adapted by scaling up or down was often used, the construction lines becoming a framework for the decorative borders, while the spaces between would be filled with decorative panels (40–47). These panels could be of finer materials and were sometimes prefabricated in a specialist centre, while the borders and surrounds were locally produced.

A series of mosaic pavements laid at Fishbourne Roman Palace, Sussex, in AD 75–80 are among the earliest in Roman Britain, and were clearly the work of mosaicists from Gaul (i.e. modern France with an area to the north reaching as far as the Rhine) or Italy (40). In the second century, following a visit by Hadrian in AD 121–2 which stimulated a demand for coloured mosaic floors to furnish the townhouses of a new class of officials, workshops grew up in St Albans, Colchester, Leicester, Cirencester and elsewhere (36–37, 40–45, 54–56), each developing characteristic motifs and styles.

In the third century there was in Britain, as elsewhere in the western Empire, a decline in crafts generally and few mosaic pavements were produced. There was, however, a revival in the fourth century when the workshops, even when situated in places where they had operated before, produced rather different designs, with more figurative motifs (46–47, 49, 51, 57).

Furniture and textiles (16–17, 62, 71, 90)

Furniture did not readily survive the destruction of Pompeii and Herculaneum, being made of lighter and inflammable materials. It is assumed, however, on evidence such as depictions of interiors in painting and sculpture, that Roman houses were lightly furnished, the main features perhaps being couches, tables and lampstands (16–17, 62).

It is also assumed that textiles must have played a role in furnishing, particularly in parts of the Empire where protection from the cold was important. Patterned materials used in clothing are sometimes indicated in sculpture, as for example on a gilt silver pepperpot from the Hoxne Treasure (71) or on funerary monuments at Palmyra (90). These patterns are clearly very similar to contemporary ornament in other media. It may well be that textile designs were fashion leaders. Textiles of all qualities and styles could move freely along the trade routes both inside and outside the frontiers. Ornamented textiles were imported into the Empire itself – Chinese silks, for example, and woollen cloth from northern Europe, the latter famous for its chequered patterns produced in plain or twill weaves.

Silver and bronze (66–76, 86)

In the Roman world it was common for prosperous households to own sets of eating and drinking vessels of silver; ceremonial plate was also owned by temples and public bodies. The quantity in use is only slightly reflected in what has been recovered, for silver was melted down and constantly reused. Occasionally, however, hoards of silver and gold which had been hidden in times of danger were not retrieved by their original owners and remained in the ground to be found in more recent times. A number of these hoards has been found in Britain and many illustrations here are taken from objects in them.

The treasure from Mildenhall, Suffolk, was deposited sometime around AD 360. It consists of over thirty items of richly decorated silver tableware, of which the most impressive piece is the Great Dish, 605 mm in diameter and weighing 8.256 kg. In the centre is the head of Oceanus (66) surrounded by revellers at some Bacchic feast. The Thetford Treasure, a hoard of jewellery, silver spoons and strainers, was found at Gallows Hill, Thetford, Norfolk, and dates from the late fourth century AD (67 CENTRE, 69, 91). There are thirty-three spoons in the hoard, many with Latin inscriptions – some bear personal names, while others relate to a cult of Faunus (a pastoral Roman god). Also present, however, are Celtic epithets and names of Celtic gods, which may suggest that Faunus was also worshipped by Celtic people. Faunus was an earth deity concerned with the land and with the protection and fertility of herds and flocks of domestic animals. His closeness to Pan is illustrated by the use of the word 'fauns' to describe creatures which, like satyrs and Pan himself, are prominent in Bacchus's entourage – as is, apparently, the panther portrayed on one of the spoons. No figure of Faunus is found in the archaeological evidence in Britain, but he may be represented by the many figures of Pan and by the satyrs which appear in representations of Bacchic worship (74). The fish depicted on another spoon (69) is unlikely in this context to be a Christian symbol.

Only one of the fourth-century hoards, from Water Newton, Huntingdonshire, can be interpreted as being the hidden treasure of a Christian community. Many of the nearly thirty silver objects in the hoard bear the *chi-rho* monogram signifying the name of Christ (71 RIGHT). The presence of the *chi-rho* alone does not, however, necessarily indicate Christianity.

A treasure found at Hoxne, Suffolk, which was deposited in the early fifth century AD, could because of its extraordinary wealth have comprised the most valuable possessions of a noble family. It consists of 29 pieces of gold jewellery, 98 spoons and other silver utensils or containers for the table, 565 gold and over 14,000 silver coins (67 ABOVE and below, 70–71 LEFT, 90 BELOW).

A silver hoard from Traprain Law, East Lothian, Scotland, is of a different kind in that all the 20 kg of silver are scrap metal. There are also four silver coins in the hoard which date to *c.* AD 400. It is assumed that hoards like this were destined to be melted down, or that the pieces of cut silver would be used as bullion by weight. The fragments of tableware, church plate, toilet sets and military equipment in the Traprain Treasure are of very high quality, and some bear traces of gilding (68). On other fragments patterns are incised or stamped with patterned and textured punches, and inlaid with niello (72). (Niello is a silver sulphide which hardens on heating and can be polished to a smooth black finish.)

Common to all the luxury goods of silver and gold is the traditional nature of the decoration. No single motif occurs that was not a part of the Hellenistic metalworking tradition, a tradition which was adopted for use by the Romans. The principal sources of silver ore in the Greek and Hellenistic world continued to be worked in the Roman period. In the west, Spain became the richest silver-producing province, although it was mined elsewhere – in Derbyshire, for example, as a by-product of lead. Analyses of Roman silver demonstrate a purity of between 92 and 98 per cent (sterling silver is 92.5 per cent). Vessels can be shaped or raised from a silver sheet by hammering to produce smooth, fluted or scalloped shapes, the latter particularly characteristic of late Roman silverware (86). On Roman vessels the marks of the hammer have normally been removed by polishing on the lathe. Additional parts, handles for example, were soldered onto the body using alloys of silver, copper and tin which had melting points well below that of the silver. Pieces could also be riveted together. The main method of producing decoration in relief, then as now, was repoussé work. In this technique an object is placed face down on a bed of soft pitch which supports the metal and yet yields as the design is beaten into it from the back. Another technique is chasing, where the surface is hammered to lower the background, thus leaving the design standing proud. Light decoration was applied by scratching the surface with a pointed tool, while engraving was done with a V-sectioned blade, gouging out a strip of metal. The head of Oceanus which decorates the centre of the Great Dish in the Mildenhall Treasure (66) was produced by a combination of all these techniques. Punches and stamps were used to construct motifs and produce repeat patterns (72–73). A multicoloured effect was achieved by gilding certain areas and by applying niello in engraved channels (1, 67, 72–73, 95).

Bronze was used for many everyday things – pots, pans, fittings for boxes, belts, brooches, armour, harness and so on (1, 65, 93–95, 98–99). Bronze figures and statuary were required for official and religious purposes and many small figures in bronze were also a part of the domestic scene (76).

Bronze is an alloy of copper and tin in which the percentage of tin does not exceed 13.2 per cent. The addition of lead makes the alloy more suitable for casting. Brass is an alloy of copper and zinc and was used by the Romans mainly for coins. Pewter is an alloy of lead and tin and was used throughout the Roman world mainly as a solder, except in Britain where it was also used for plates and vessels.

The usual method for casting in silver or bronze was by the lost wax method. A model of the object was made in wax and was then surrounded by a layer of clay. When heated, the wax would melt and run away through a hole in the clay coating which would itself be baked hard. Molten metal was then poured through the hole into what was now a mould of burnt clay. When cool, the clay mould would be broken to reveal the metal object, which was then finished and polished.

Large objects and figures were hollow cast. A clay core was built up to the approximate finished shape and covered with an outer skin of wax. This in turn was built up to the thickness of the desired metal wall and the finer details were modelled on the outer wax surface. The whole was covered, as already described, with a clay jacket and metal pins were inserted to hold the core in place. When heated, the wax melted and a mould was produced into which the melted bronze could be poured. For complicated figures several pieces were cast separately and assembled later.

These methods did not lend themselves to mass production, and piece-mould casting was used for most of the small utilitarian objects which were produced by the thousand. By this method a mould of the complete object was prepared in clay or stone. A simple core was inserted for each casting, leaving the thickness of the bronze more uneven than with the lost wax method. These moulds could be used again and again.

Bronze sheet was produced and could be raised to form vessels. Decorated bronze sheet was also used to cover belts, boxes, scabbards etc. (94–95). This was often decorated in repoussé, whereby the sheet metal was hammered onto a die in which the decoration had been cut in reverse. Brooches and military bronzes were often tinned, as were the insides of some vessels used for cooking.

Glass (77)

Glass was known in the ancient world from about the middle of the third millennium BC. In Greece glass was made in the middle of the fifth century, while in the fourth century Syria became an important centre for glass making. Later, Alexandria was the dominant centre of production. In early times vessels and objects of glass were made by applying molten glass to a pre-formed core and by moulding and grinding glass blocks. The time and place of the invention of glass blowing is not known, but it is likely to have occurred in the Syrian coastal area in the first century BC. Glass blowing transformed the glass industry and, by the late first century AD, blown glass had almost completely superseded all other methods of manufacture (save for the manufacture of beads).

The constituents of glass during the Roman period were similar to those in most periods of antiquity – a mixture of silica (i.e. sand) with about 15 per cent soda and 10 per cent lime. It was common practice to include an amount of broken glass waste (cullet) in the mixture. The addition of metal oxides produced a range of colours which also depended on the management of the furnace: copper produced dark blue or green to red colours; cobalt a rich blue; manganese yellow or purple; antimony opaque yellow, and iron pale blue, green, amber or black.

There is reason to believe that Roman blown glass was produced much as it is today. Decorative features could be produced by blowing into a patterned mould, tooling the glass while still hot or applying strands and knobs (77). Cold glass could be painted, cut or engraved. Wheel cutting, engraving and facet cutting were used throughout the Roman period. Cameo cutting was used on vessels blown from blanks of two or more coloured glasses; the outer skin, usually opaque white, was cut away to reveal the ground colour beneath. The British Museum's Portland Vase, dating from the first century BC or AD, is the most famous example of the cameo technique. Another type of vessel produced with the help of a wheel was the cage cup. Here a thick blank was cut away to produce an almost freestanding fretwork of interlocking rings or figures, the outer frame being joined to the body of the vessel by small pillars (77). An important innovation was window glass, which makes its appearance in the first century AD. Glass obviously does not travel well, and the more common forms of glass vessels were manufactured locally in many parts of the Empire.

Pottery (26–27, 78–85, 97)

Pottery is by far the most durable material to have survived from antiquity, and this is perhaps particularly true of Roman pottery, which is found in large quantities. Its survival is partly due to the excellent quality of the pottery produced by the Romans at home and abroad. The red-slipped pottery first made in Arezzo in Tuscany and known as Arretine ware was developed in response to a demand for a cheaper alternative to silver tableware. The moulded decoration clearly imitates repoussé decoration on silver, with its conventional scenes from mythology or heroic tales and with borders of leaves and flowers (26–27, 80–81). (A contemporary writer, Pliny the Elder (AD 23–79), says that plaster casts of the decoration on silver vessels were used as 'portable patterns of Greek art'. Such casts may also have been available to potters.)

Pottery with relief decoration was produced in moulds – thick clay bowls on the inside of which were impressed designs of figures, swags, garlands and borders. When baked, the mould would be used many times to produce vessels which could be finished by adding such elements as foot rings, pedestals and handles. Further figural scenes could be 'luted' on, i.e. stuck on with a little liquid clay. Workshops copying Arretine ware (whose products are sometimes known as Samian ware) were set up in western Europe; thus, for example, one manufacturer, Gnaeus Ateius, who signed the cup illustrated 81 TOP RIGHT, is known to have established workshops in Pisa and Lyons as well as in Arezzo. Other areas in western Europe with excellent potting clays, such as the Auvergne and the Rhineland, set up productions of less formal, but still high-quality pottery decorated in different techniques. A trailed slip decoration known as 'barbotine' was produced by means of a soft, almost liquid, clay which was squeezed through a nozzle onto the surface of a pot in the same way as a baker pipes icing onto a cake. At its best, this technique achieved not only scrolls and leaf designs but lively figural scenes (82–83). Vessels decorated in this manner often had less formal shapes. Pottery decoration also copied the sharp cutting designs of engraved glass (84). In addition, rollers and stamps of many kinds were all part of the potter's tool-kit. In Britain very accomplished pottery was produced – for example, at Castor in the Nene Valley near Peterborough (82 ABOVE LEFT, 83, 97). Coarse pottery like the face-pots from Colchester (85) represents the timeless production of potters at all times, everywhere.

Roman pottery was thrown on the wheel, although the precise type of wheel used is not known. Kilns of various types have been excavated in many parts of the Empire. All worked on the simple up-draught principle, in which pots were stacked above the fire, the hot gases rising past the pots and out of the top of the kiln.

The red glossy slip, which is above all characteristic of the better class of Roman pottery, fell out of use at the end of the Roman period and it has been something of a mystery how this effect was accomplished. It would appear, however, that the gloss was achieved when the slip was applied as a wash of liquid clay in which certain small particles which occur naturally in many clays were held in suspension. Ordinary clay slips – simply liquid clay – were coloured with iron and could produce surfaces in colours from red or orange to brown and black, depending on an oxidising or reducing atmosphere in the kiln.

Glazed pottery can be found in all parts of the Empire but is not common. Lead glazes were developed in Asia Minor and northern Syria in the first century BC (78). Blue or turquoise alkali silicate 'frit' glaze was used in Egypt and on the eastern fringes of the Empire (79).

Lamps and figures (23, 51, 60–62, 64–65, 76, 96)

Artificial lighting in Roman times was limited to torches – mainly out of doors because of the smoke and danger – and lamps which generally burned olive oil or, in those parts of the Empire where the olive was not cultivated or imported, candles of tallow and beeswax.

Lamps, whether of metal, pottery or stone all have a fuel chamber with a filling hole, one or more nozzles for the wick and normally a handle. They were usually made in specialist workshops. The first step in making lamps was to produce a prototype (*patrice*) of clay or some other material. This was a solid model of the basic shape of the lamp. Relief decoration would be added to the prototype at this stage. Moulds of gypsum plaster were taken from the prototype. For a simple type of lamp a mould in two halves was sufficient. Thin sheets of wet clay were pressed into each half of the mould and the halves were then joined. When the clay had hardened a little, as water was taken up by the plaster, the lamp was taken out of the mould, the filling hole and nozzles cut, and the handle pierced. Additional decoration could be applied at this stage. A slip coating completed most lamps. The lamp was then fired. This method of manufacture made it easy to copy popular models as new prototypes could be produced from existing lamps, and prototypes could be exchanged between workshops.

Lamps were a very big trading item. In the first century BC and first century AD Italian lamps were exported in large quantities. In the provinces, however, local workshops grew up which reproduced Italian lamps as well as developing their own types.

The same techniques were used in the manufacture of terracotta figurines –

cult figures of gods, goddesses and heroes (76) – though in these industries fired clay moulds were more commonly used than plaster.

Jewellery and enamelling (87–95)

The goldsmith's art changed in the course of the Roman period from the exclusive tradition of Greece and the Middle East, with its ancient and generally conservative methods and motifs, to one with simpler and more labour-saving techniques. The resulting more gaudy and inventive styles paved the way for the Byzantine art which was to follow and the art of the European Middle Ages. Gold came in the form of bars or ingots, probably originally from the Balkans but also from Gaul, Spain and Britain. Natural gold always contains silver and Roman gold rarely has less than 5 per cent. If the proportion of silver in gold rises above 20 per cent the appearance changes sufficiently for this to have been known in antiquity as 'white gold' or 'electrum'. In the production of jewellery the various components were made by casting, sheet gold and wire. Sheets were hammered to a thickness of some 0.2–0.5 mm and embossed designs were produced by repoussé and chasing; punches were employed both on the back and front of the sheet (91, 94–95). Wire was normally produced by twisting a strip of metal and rolling it between plates of stone or bronze. It was primarily used to make chains (often mistakenly described as plaited). Loop-in-loop chains are all made from links, each an oval ring bent into a U-shape and threaded through the looped ends of the next link (89).

The gaudy multicoloured enamelling which had developed among the Celtic tribes on the edges of the Roman world continued to be popular amongst their conquered descendants. By the last quarter of the first century AD enamelled brooches were produced in large numbers in the Roman world. Among British examples Celtic motifs are sometimes found, but most are in a Roman provincial style. Throughout the second and into the third century, enamelled trinkets, brooches, rings and studs were produced in Britain and Gaul and exported both to the east as far as Syria and beyond the Roman frontiers to the north.

Enamel is a glassy substance fused to a metallic base. The glass could be mixed with metallic oxides for colouring. The usual method, champlevé, involved placing the pulverised glass (frit) into cells which had been cast or built up on a metal base. There would usually be just one colour to each cell. On heating, the frit would melt, fill the cell and adhere to the metal. Millefiori, a multicoloured pattern in enamelling, was produced like a stick of seaside rock. Glass rods of different colours were fused together; when the resultant stick was sliced it produced plaques of patterned glass which could be set in cells (92).

The extremely conservative nature of Roman decoration is apparent in this collection of designs. Of all the many innovations introduced by the Romans, new motifs in decorative art were not much in evidence. It is indeed striking that only a narrow range of motifs was adapted to all areas of applied art. Real changes began to take place when a different artistic tradition met and mingled with that of the Romans along the northern frontiers of the Empire. The Germanic peoples of northern Germany and Scandinavia had a lively contact with the Empire, serving in its army and eventually contributing to its fall. These people took motifs such as Oceanus between dolphins, spirals, scrolls and palmettes, and broke them up by faceting so that they caught the light and created exciting uncertainties, far removed from the predictable order which was the strength, as well as the weakness, of Roman art (98–99).

In Britain the art of the Anglo-Saxons reveals both Celtic and Germanic artistic traditions and flair, but much of the Roman decorative heritage was also retained. Major motifs of Roman art survived for centuries in Europe. Motifs such as the eagle, acanthus and leaf scroll and the vase-and-flower appear in the high art of the medieval Romanesque and the Renaissance, as well as in popular folk tradition. In decorative art, as in many other areas of civilised life, the heritage of the Romans in Europe pervades our culture to this day.

Notes on the Designs

NB In this book, the colours of mosaics are indicated in the drawings by tints or stippling. Black represents the darkest element in the design, which can be black or dark shades of grey or brown. A medium shade often indicates red, while the lighter shade may be yellow. Note that the background may not be totally white but in local stone of a cream colour, as at Chedworth (33). In many instances the actual colours are described in the individual entry. In some designs individual stones of the background colour have not been indicated.

The grids in this collection of designs suggest practical methods of construction only. Other grids could in most cases equally well be used. There is, as a rule, no evidence of the methods used in antiquity.

1 *British Museum* PRB 1893.6–18.14. Length of handle 140 mm.

2 ABOVE Temple of Mater Matuta, Satricum (Conca, near Anzio, late 6th–early 5th centuries BC. Height 300 mm. Painted in cream, with red and black borders. Villa Giulia, Rome. Andrén, A. 1939–40, *Architectural Terracottas from Etrusco-Italic Temples*, Svenska Institutet i Rom Skrifter, VI, Lund and Leipzig, pl. 152:517. CENTRE Sassi Caduti, Etruria, 5th century BC. Height 240 mm. Painted in white, red and black. Villa Giulia, Rome. Andrén op. cit., pl. 39:129. BELOW Lo Scasato (temple area), Etruria, 3rd century BC. Height 450 mm. Painted in white, red and black. *Villa Giulia*, Rome. This design occurs on many other sites and was in use from the 4th century BC onwards. Andrén op. cit., pl. 54:173.

3 ABOVE This design of openwork cresting occurs on several sites. This example is from the Temple of Jupiter, Cosa, Etruria, 3rd–2nd centuries BC. Brown, F.E., Richardson, E.H. and Richardson, L. Jr. 1960, *Cosa II, The Temple of the Arx*, Memoir of the American Academy in Rome, XXVI, fig. 14, pl. xviii, 1. BELOW Fragment of a terracotta plaque found in Rome during excavations for the Via dell'Impero. Red and black paint on a cream ground. *Antiquarium Communale*, Rome. Andrén op. cit., pl. 109:389.

4 ABOVE Two painted borders in tombs at Thebes, Egypt: LEFT no.75, tomb of Amenhotpe-si-se; RIGHT no.90, tomb of Nebamun. New Kingdom, 18th Dynasty (c.1425–1379). Wilson, E. 1986, *Ancient Egyptian Designs*, British Museum Pattern Books, London, p. 57. CENTRE Three painted borders on pottery from Athens,

Greece: LEFT from Vulci, Etruria, 520–500 BC, RIGHT and BELOW from Camirus, Rhodes, 580 BC. *British Museum*, Vases B 331, B 76. BELOW Detail of a relief design on a terracotta plaque. Temple of Mater Matuta, Satricum (Conca, near Anzio), third quarter of the 6th century BC. Height of border c.180 mm. *Villa Giulia*, Rome. Andrén op. cit., pl. 139:488.

5 ABOVE Sassi Caduti, Etruria, 5th century BC. Height of border c. 180 mm. Painted in white, red and black. *Villa Giulia*, Rome. CENTRE Temple of Juno Sospita, Lanuvium, Latium (Lazio), late 6th–first half of 5th century BC. Height of border c. 160 mm. Painted in white, red and black on a cream slip. *British Museum*. BELOW Sassi Caduti, Etruria, 5th century BC. Height of border c. 210 mm. Painted in white, red and black. *Villa Giulia*, Rome. Andrén op. cit., ABOVE pl. 40:132; CENTRE pl. 131:458; BELOW pl. 43:141.

6 ABOVE *British Museum*, GR 1860.2–1.16. CENTRE LEFT *British Museum*, Vases B 310, E 171. CENTRE RIGHT *Lady Lever Art Gallery*, Port Sunlight, no.54. BELOW Height of border c. 245 mm. *Museo dell'Opera del Duomo*, Orvieto. Andrén op. cit., pl. 63:204.

7 ABOVE Temple of Juno Sospita, Lanuvium. Height of border c. 600 mm. *British Museum*, Terracotta D 711. BELOW Height of border c. 300 mm. *Villa Giulia*, Rome. Andrén op. cit., pl. 119:423.

8 ABOVE Detail from the bronze casket known as the 'Ficoroni cista' found in Palestrina (Praeneste). Made in Rome by Novios Plautios, second half of 4th century BC. *Villa Giulia*, Rome. Dohrn, T. 1972, *Die Ficoronische Ciste in der Villa Giulia in Rom*, Monumenta Artis Romanae, XI, Taf. 15.

CENTRE Orvieto, Via degli Alberici, 2nd–1st centuries BC. Height 170 mm. *Museo dell'Opera del Duomo*, Orvieto. Andrén op. cit., pl. 75:257. BELOW Mid-1st century BC–mid-2nd century AD. *Museo Nazionale*, Naples. Borbein, A.H. 1968, *Campana Reliefs*, Heidelberg, Taf. 35.

9 ABOVE LEFT No colouring remains on this plaque except on the bottom border where the palmettes are white against a red ground. 1st century BC. Height 750 mm. *Villa Giulia*, Rome. Andrén op. cit., pl. 134:470. ABOVE RIGHT The Monumental Arch, Palmyra. BELOW Temple of Apollo, Didyma: panel at base of column 7. *On site.*

10 FROM THE LEFT (1) Example of the Greek Doric Order. Known as the Theseum, Athens, mid-5th century BC. (2) Example of the Greek Ionic Order. Temple of Ilissus, Athens, 484 BC. Destroyed in 1780 (reconstructed). (3) Example of the Roman Ionic Order. Temple of Fortuna Virilis, Rome, 100 BC. Converted in 880 to the church S. Maria Egiziaca. After Fletcher, Sir Banister, 1931, *A History of Architecture on the comparative method*, London, 9th edn, first published 1896, pp. 95, 103, 105, 122, 150–51.

11 ABOVE Detail from the anta-capital in the East Porch of the Erechtheion, Athens. *British Museum*, Sculpture 409. BELOW (1) Detail from marble door frame. Eumachia building, the Forum, Pompeii, 1st century AD. (2) Temple of Bel, Palmyra, Syria, 1st century AD. *On site.* (3) San Lorenzo fuori le Mura, Rome, late 2nd century AD.

12 ABOVE Detail from the anta-capital in the East Porch of the Erechtheion, Athens, late 5th century BC. *British Museum*, Sculpture 409. BELOW (1)

Domitian Villa, Castel Gandolfo, 81–96 AD. *Villa Barberini*, Rome. (2) The Nymphaeum, Jerash, Syria, 2nd century AD. *On site*.

13 LEFT The Choragic Monument of Lysicrates, Athens, 335 BC. The monument was erected to support a tripod at Greek festivals. TOP CENTRE Capital on the Tower of the Winds, Athens, 100–35 BC. This small building measured the time by means of a water-clock and sundial. It also had a weather vane. CENTRE Pilaster capital from the Pantheon in the Campus Martius, Rome, AD 118–28. *British Museum*, Sculptures 2592 and 2594. BELOW CENTRE Corinthian capital. Temple of Castor and Pollux, Rome, 1st century AD. 14.76 m high. RIGHT Example of the Roman Corinthian Order. The Pantheon, Rome, AD 120–24. Unfluted monolithic column of marble and granite with Corinthian capital of white Pentelic marble. 14.15 m high. All except CENTRE after Fletcher op. cit., LEFT 114, 122; TOP CENTRE 111, 112, 114, 117; RIGHT 122, 161; BELOW CENTRE 150, 155.

14 ABOVE Drawing by Marjorie Blamey. CENTRE Reconstructed design from the top of a marble stele made in Athens. *British Museum*, Sculpture 605. BELOW *British Museum*, GR 1921.12–20.125.

15 *Ara Pacis Augustae*, Rome. 13 BC–AD 9. This monumental altar was voted by the Senate to celebrate Augustus' return from Spain and Gaul and the peace that followed. The monument has many figurative panels, as well as those with elaborate acanthus designs.

16 ABOVE Terracotta plaque, Rome, made in Italy 30 BC–AD 20. *British Museum*. BELOW Motif repeated on three sides of the base of a marble candelabra. Length of motif *c*. 500 mm. *British Museum*, Sculpture 2509.

17 LEFT *British Museum*, Sculpture 2606. RIGHT Drawing based on sketches. *British Museum*, Sculpture 2509.

18 FROM THE TOP (1) Palmyra, Syria. Temple of Bel (dedicated AD 32). Detail of one of several borders which decorate the frame of the door to the peristyle. (2) Design of rosettes in a scroll border reconstructed from funerary monuments in *Palmyra Museum*. Valley of the Tombs, first half of 3rd century AD. (3) Detail of an acanthus scroll in mosaic from the 'Great Pavement' at Woodchester, Gloucestershire, *c*. AD 300–325. Leaves are alternately brown and cream with black outlines; the main curving stem has a red centre. *British Museum*, PRB 1808.2–27.1. (4) Stylised acanthus scroll from Hinton St Mary, Dorset, 4th century AD. Outlined in black, the leaves are red with a yellow centre. *British Museum*.

19 ABOVE LEFT and RIGHT Details from the 'Months and Seasons' mosaic. *British Museum*, Mosaic 29. BELOW LEFT Detail from a mosaic panel found on the site of the Bank of England. 3rd century AD. *British Museum*.

20 FROM THE TOP (1) Apulia, Italy, 370–360 BC. *British Museum*, Vase F 160. (2) Engraved design on a silver platter. Stráze, Slovakia. (3) Detail from mosaic, Abbots Ann, Andover, Hampshire. Black and red on white. *British Museum*, PRB 1854.6–23.1.

21 TOP LEFT ABOVE Motif from the 'Hunting Dog' mosaic, Dyer Street, Cirencester, Gloucestershire, 2nd century AD. *Corinium Museum*, Cirencester. TOP LEFT BELOW Ivy motif from the 'Dolphins and Fountain' mosaic, Verulamium, Hertfordshire, *c*. AD 145–50. *Verulamium Museum*, St Albans. Detail of design in rectangular panel. Black outline, leaves white, yellow and red. TOP RIGHT Palmyra, Syria. Valley of the Tombs, 1st–2nd century AD. Border design in relief from funerary monuments. *Palmyra Museum*. BELOW Two border designs from mosaics at Roman Carthage, Tunisia, North

Africa, 4th–5th centuries AD. *British Museum*, Mosaics 49b and 29. The ribbon design is white, yellow and light brown on the underside and white, pink and red on the outside. The flower is shaded in white and grey.

22 Ais-es-Salmani, near Benghazi, Cyrenaica, Libya, North Africa. *British Museum*, Sarcophagus 37.

23 Clay lamps made in Italy. ABOVE About AD 50–100, diameter 250 mm. CENTRE LEFT First half of 1st century AD, 98 × 72 mm. On base ring North Italian maker's name T. CELER with workshop probably at Tortona. CENTRE RIGHT Third quarter of 1st century AD, 131 × 84 mm. BELOW Late 1st century BC or early 1st century AD, 98 × 85 mm. *British Museum*, Q1103, Q788, Q971, Q850.

24 ABOVE LEFT Coptic Egypt, 4th–5th centuries AD. Tapestry woven band in wool and linen on linen. *Victoria and Albert Museum*, London. CENTRE Coptic Egypt, 3rd–4th centuries AD. Head of Dionysus, woven in linen and wool. *Textile Museum*, Washington. ABOVE RIGHT From Temple of Bel, Palmyra, Syria, 1st century AD (dedicated AD 32). (1) Detail of one of several borders which decorate the frame of a door in the peristyle. (2) Detail from monument in the Grave Temple, 2nd century AD. *On site*. BELOW Engraved design on silver vase. Hoxne, Suffolk, late 4th–early 5th centuries AD. Actual height of border *c*. 30 mm. *British Museum*, PRB P.1994.4–8.31.

25 FROM THE TOP (1) Palmyra, Syria. Valley of the Tombs, 1st–2nd centuries AD. Border design from a funerary monument. *Palmyra Museum*. (2) Relief in stone. Gandhara, 2nd–3rd centuries AD. Height 140 mm. *British Museum*, OA 1951.5–8.1. (3) Border motif from the Middleborough Mosaic, Colchester, Essex, AD 175. *Castle Museum*, Colchester. (4) Sidon, Lebanon, 3rd century AD. Moulded motif

from a lead coffin. *British Museum*, 1921.12–13.2.

26–27 From Oswald, F. and Pryce, T.D. 1920, *An Introduction to the Study of Terra Sigillata treated from a Chronological Standpoint*, London. Provincial Roman pottery designs, 1st century AD. **26** FROM THE TOP (1) Pl. VIII, 3. Sandy, Bedfordshire. Made in La Graufesenque district, near Toulouse, France, *c*. AD 50. Height 120 mm. *British Museum*. (2–4) Pl. XXXI, 26, 32, 38. **27** FROM THE TOP Pl. XXXI, 21, 23, 24, 40, 31.

28 Demonstration drawings.

29 FROM THE TOP (1) Border motif from the 'Great Fan' mosaic at Verulamium, Hertfordshire, 2nd century AD. *Verulamium Museum*, St Albans. (2) Border motif from mosaic at Masada, Israel, 1st century AD. *On site*. (3) Aldborough, York, 2nd century AD. *Aldborough Museum*. (4) Top of the Dionysian frieze, Villa of the Mysteries, Pompeii, Italy, 80 BC–AD 14.

30 ABOVE LEFT Priene, Ionia, Turkey, *c*. 330–300 BC. Silver coin. Diameter 18 mm. *British Museum*, BMC Priene 2. CENTRE LEFT Knossos, Crete, *c*. 400–350 BC. Silver coin. Diameter 21.5 mm. *British Museum*, BMC 5. CENTRE RIGHT Knossos, Crete, 4th century BC. Silver coin. Diameter 24 mm. *British Museum*, 1896.7.3.308. ABOVE RIGHT Painted decoration inside a bowl. Made in Athens, found at Vulci, Etruria, Italy, 440–430 BC. *British Museum*, Vase E 84. BELOW Floor design in the House of the Labyrinth, Room 42, Pompeii, 60–70 BC. Laid in black and white tesserae with a multicoloured design in the centre showing Theseus fighting the Minotaur. The labyrinth is not open at the centre. It is 2.06 m square, which is the equivalent of 7 Roman feet. Strocka, V.M. 1991, *Casa del Libirinto*, Deutsches Archaeologisches Institut, 'Häuser in Pompeji', Band 4, Munich. Quotation from Smith, D.J. 1959, 'The Labyrinth at Caerleon', *Board of Celtic Studies Bulletin* 18, 3.

31 ABOVE Demonstration drawings. BELOW Mosaic designs from Antioch, Turkey. LEFT House of Trajan Aqueduct; RIGHT House of Iphigenia. 2nd century AD.

32 ABOVE Rockbourne, Hampshire, late 3rd century AD. Laid in dark grey and white tesserae. *On site.* BELOW From the columns in the garden of the Villa of the Mosaic Columns, Pompeii, mid–1st century AD. *Naples Museum.*

33 ABOVE From a mosaic pavement at Fullerton, Hampshire, 4th century AD. *Fullerton Manor.* BELOW The design of a mosaic pavement in Room 14, Chedworth Roman Villa, Gloucestershire, 4th century AD. Chedworth mosaics are laid with tesserae of local stone and tile. Pure limestone for white – or rather a light cream colour – Liassic limestone containing iron for blue and grey, and Forest of Dean sandstone for purple. Cubes of pottery tile for bright red. This design is in cream, blue and red.

34 Floor design from the Temple of Apollo, Pompeii, 1st century BC–1st century AD. Each lozenge 125 mm side. Pale green limestone, grey slate, white palombine marble. *On site.*

35 ABOVE House of the Labyrinth, Room 40, Pompeii, 1st century BC. See Strocka op. cit., see **30**. Floor in lattice pattern set with tesserae, white criss-cross lines, centre diamond black, sides in alternate rows red and green/yellow. Diamonds 220 × 110 mm. CENTRE and BELOW Floor designs, Antioch, Turkey, 2nd century AD.

36–37 The Blackfriar's Pavement, Leicester, *c.* AD 150. *Jewry Wall Museum,* Leicester. The tesserae in this mosaic are local grey and white Liassic limestone or carboniferous limestone from Derbyshire, while the brown and red colours in the centre of the roundels and in the border are ironstone from eastern

Leicestershire and broken tile or pottery.

38 ABOVE LEFT Motif from the 'Hunting Dog' mosaic, Dyer Street, Cirencester, Gloucestershire, 2nd century AD. *Corinium Museum,* Cirencester. CENTRE Rockbourne, Hampshire. East Bath Suite, early 4th century AD. Brown and red on pure white. *On site.* ABOVE RIGHT Silchester, Hampshire. Detail from a mosaic pavement in a courtyard house (block XIV) by the Calleva workshop, AD 140–60. Outline black with red and cream petals on white. BELOW The swastika-pelta design, based on an intersecting circles grid, is common from the 2nd to the 4th centuries AD. This example is from Verulamium, Hertfordshire. *Verulamium Museum,* St Albans.

39 FROM THE TOP (1) The simple twist could be taken from any number of mosaic pavements. This, like the angular form beneath it (2), comes from the 'Venus' mosaic, Kingscote, Gloucestershire, late 3rd to early 4th centuries AD. *Corinium Museum,* Cirencester. Colours are alternately black-red-yellow-black and black-blue-green-black. (3) Detail of the border of a mosaic panel from the site of the Bank of England, 3rd century AD. *British Museum.* Note the colour distribution does not create the illusion of a realistic ribbon. Sequence black-white-yellow-red-black. (4) A ring-chain border design. Carthage, mid-2nd century AD. *British Museum,* Mosaic 18. Colour distribution, light ribbon: black-white-light and dark olive brown-black; dark ribbon: black-white-pink-red-black.

40 Fishbourne, Sussex, *c.* AD 75–80. Detail of mosaic from Rooms N 12 and 7. Grids after Field, R. 1988, *Patterns from Roman Mosaics,* Diss.

41 North Hill, Colchester, second half of 2nd century AD. *Castle Museum,* Colchester. This design can be drawn with the

help of a square grid with a diagonal grid superimposed. The regular octagons are created when the spaces of the grid alternate, the wider being one third larger than the narrower. Neal, D.S. 1981, *Roman Mosaics in Britain. An Introduction to Their Schemes and a Catalogue of Paintings,* Britannia Monograph Series, 1, London, p. 22.

42–43 The 'Dahlia' mosaic pavement, Verulamium, Hertfordshire, 2nd century AD. *Verulamium Museum,* St Albans. Grid after Neal, op. cit., p. 23.

44–45 The 'Cernunnus' mosaic, Verulamium, Hertfordshire, 2nd century AD. *Verulamium Museum,* St Albans.

46 Suggested guide lines or grid for the construction of the central panel of the 'Venus' mosaic pavement from Kingscote, Gloucestershire, late 3rd or early 4th centuries AD. *Corinium Museum,* Cirencester.

47 Details of motifs in the Kingscote mosaic. The tail of the lower dolphin is reconstructed in the drawing.

48 ABOVE Border design from the 'Cupid and Dolphin' mosaic, Fishbourne, Sussex, *c.* AD 160. CENTRE LEFT Detail from the 'Lion Mosaic' at Verulamium, Hertfordshire, *c.* AD 180. *Verulamium Museum,* St Albans. CENTRE RIGHT Detail from a mosaic pavement in Building VI, 4, Admiral's Walk, Cirencester, Gloucestershire, ?3rd century AD. *Corinium Museum,* Cirencester. BELOW The threshold panel of the 'Hare' mosaic from Building XII, 1, Beeches Road, Cirencester, 3rd–4th centuries AD. *Corinium Museum,* Cirencester.

49 Hinton St Mary, Dorset, first half of 4th century AD. *British Museum.*

50 ABOVE Cylinder seal impression. Mesopotamia, *c.* 2334–2193 BC. *British Museum,* WA 89308. CENTRE Motif from a jug made in the Cyclades. Aegina, Greece, *c.* 675–650 BC. *British Museum*

GR 1873.8–20, 385. BELOW Motif on a terracotta plaque, Melos, Greece, 460–430 BC. *British Museum,* Terracotta 616.

51 ABOVE Detail of mosaic in Lullingstone Roman Villa, Kent, mid-4th century AD. *On site.* BELOW LEFT Mould-made lamp of buff clay, first third of 1st century AD. 94 × 73 mm. *British Museum,* Q767. BELOW RIGHT Mould-made lamp of buff clay, first third of 1st century AD. 117 × 84 mm. *British Museum,* Q784.

52 ABOVE Design on Samian ware. Central Gaul, *c.* AD 100–200. After Stanfield, J.A. and Simpson, G. 1958, *Central Gaulish Potters,* London, pl. 26, no. 319). CENTRE and BELOW Silver hoard buried AD 410–25. The Traprain Treasure, Traprain Law, East Lothian, Scotland, late 4th–early 5th century AD. *National Museums of Scotland,* Edinburgh. From the fragmentary bowl no.36. From Curle, A.O. 1923, *The Treasure of Traprain,* Glasgow.

53 The Mildenhall Treasure, Mildenhall, Suffolk, 4th century AD. Design on a silver flanged bowl. Diameter 268 mm. *British Museum,* PRB 1946.10–7.7.

54 Fishbourne Roman Palace, Chichester, Sussex. Motifs from the 'Cupid on a Dolphin' mosaic in Room F. Laid *c.* AD 160 on top of an earlier mosaic with a mainly geometric design (see detail **40** BELOW).

55 Two motifs from the 'Hunting Dog' mosaic, found in Dyer Street, Cirencester, Gloucestershire. 2nd century AD. *Corinium Museum,* Cirencester.

56 ABOVE Verulamium, Hertfordshire, *c.* AD 145–59. Motif from 'Dolphins and Vase' (cantharus) fountain. *Verulamium Museum,* St Albans. Cantharus in black, white, yellow and red. Dolphin body white-grey-black with fins in black and red. Water spray grey. BELOW Roman Carthage, North Africa, second half of 4th century AD. Detail from the border of the 'Months and Seasons' mosaic. Height of panel 500 mm. The bodies of the dolphins are shaded in blue and green with black outline. Red and cream mouth and fin details. *British Museum*, Mosaic 29.

57 Chedworth Roman Villa, Gloucestershire, Room 5, 4th century AD. The colours are strong and dark on a light cream ground. Chedworth mosaics are laid with tesserae of local stone and tile (see **33**).

58 Halicarnassos, Anatolia (Bodrum, Turkey), 4th century AD. Motifs from mosaics. *British Museum*, Mosaics 54, 56.

59 Halicarnassos, Anatolia (Bodrum, Turkey), 4th century AD. Motifs from a mosaic. *British Museum*, Mosaic 54.

60 ABOVE Made in Italy, 1st century BC. Height 232 mm. *British Museum*, Terracotta D 690. BELOW LEFT Italy, said to be from Pozzuoli, c. AD 50–90. 143 × 92 mm. BELOW RIGHT Made in Italy, AD 50–100. 157 × 107 mm. *British Museum*, Q948, Q957.

61 ABOVE Carthage, Tunisia, c. AD 200. 124 × 86 mm. By the lamp-maker Augendus. BELOW LEFT No provenance, c. AD 50–80. 121 × 103 mm. BELOW RIGHT Tunisia, AD 175–225. 138 × 105 mm. Signed by the lamp-maker Augendus. *British Museum*, Q1715, Q1203, Q1700.

62 Pompeii, House of Paquinus Proculus, second half of 1st century AD. Bronze lamp, 195 × 90 mm.

63 Temple of Sulis Minerva, Bath, 1st century AD. Stone relief of Gorgon's head on the pediment.

64 ABOVE Sketch of motif in light relief from marble altar, 1st century AD. Approximate size of motif 200 × 250 mm. No provenance. *British Museum*, Sculpture 2493. CENTRE Sketch of motif in light relief from marble tomb-chest, 1st century AD. Approximate length of motif 350 mm. No provenance. *British Museum*, Sculpture 2376. BELOW LEFT Cyrenaica, Libya, 2nd century AD. 97 × 80 mm. BELOW RIGHT Central Italy, first half of 2nd

century AD. 107 × 79 mm. *British Museum*, Q1875, Q1310.

65 ABOVE Nocera, Campania, Italy, 1st century AD. Bronze, 163 × 78 mm. There is a second hole at the back of the head. CENTRE LEFT Mould-made lamp of buff clay, handle broken. Probably late 1st century BC. 96 × 70 mm. CENTRE RIGHT Bronze, c. 1st century AD. Length 95 mm. BELOW Mould-made clay lamp. No provenance, c. AD 40–80. 177 × 80 mm. *British Museum*, Q3596, Q742, Q3581, Q1010.

66 Diameter of the design c. 100 mm. *British Museum*, PRB 1946.10–7.1.

67 ABOVE and BELOW The Hoxne Treasure, Hoxne, Suffolk, late 4th–early 5th centuries AD. ABOVE Length of bowl 85 mm. BELOW Length 115 mm. *British Museum*, PRB P.1994.4–8.62 and 64. CENTRE The Thetford Treasure, Gallows Hill, Thetford, Norfolk, late 4th century AD. Length 102 mm. *British Museum*, PRB P.1981.2–1,50. Drawings after Philip Compton in Johns, C. and Potter, T. 1983, *The Thetford Treasure, Roman Jewellery and Silver*, London.

68 ABOVE The Traprain Treasure, Traprain Law, East Lothian, Scotland, late 4th–early 5th century AD. Central motif of bowl no. 30. *National Museums of Scotland*, Edinburgh. From Curle op. cit. (see **52**).

69 The Thetford Treasure, Gallows Hill, Thetford, Norfolk, late 4th century AD. FROM THE TOP (1) Silver strainer and pick. Length 150 mm. (2) Silver spoon with parcel gilding. Inscribed DEIIFAVNI-NARI. Length 177 mm. (3) Silver spoon. Length 178 mm. (4) Silver spoon with inscription AGRESTEVIVAS. Length 183 mm. *British Museum*, PRB P.1981.2–1, 4, 49, 66, 67 and 72. Drawings after Philip Compton in Johns and Potter op. cit. (see **67**).

70 The Hoxne Treasure, Hoxne, Suffolk, late 4th–early 5th centuries AD. FROM THE TOP

(1, 2) Silver ladles. Length c. 140 mm and 148 mm. The ladle ABOVE is gilded. (3) Silver ear- and tooth-pick with gilding and niello. Length 145 mm. *British Museum*, PRB P.1994.4–8.42, 52, 146.

71 TOP LEFT The Hoxne Treasure, Hoxne, Suffolk, late 4th–early 5th centuries AD. Silver-gilt pepperpot. Height 103 mm. RIGHT Water Newton, Huntingdonshire, 4th century AD. Silver strainer. Length 202 mm. BELOW The Mildenhall Treasure, Mildenhall, Suffolk, 4th century AD. Length 152 mm. *British Museum*, PRB P.1994.4–8.33, P.1975.10–2.9, 1946.10–7.18–26.

72 The Traprain Treasure, Traprain Law, East Lothian, Scotland, late 4th or early 5th centuries AD. *National Museums of Scotland*, Edinburgh. ABOVE Design on a fragment from the rim of dish no. 68. Actual width of border c. 25 mm. BELOW Three details of designs on flagon 4. Actual width of borders from the top, c. 20 mm, 15 mm and 25 mm. From Curle op. cit. (see **52**).

73 The Mildenhall Treasure, Mildenhall, Suffolk, 4th century AD. *British Museum*, PRB 1946.10–7.4. Details of the design in the centre and round the rim of a large silver dish. Diameter 556 mm; roundel diameter c. 115 mm; border width c. 30 mm.

74 The Mildenhall Treasure, Mildenhall, Suffolk, 4th century AD. Design on a silver platter. Diameter 185 mm. *British Museum*, PRB 1946.10–7.3.

75 LEFT and RIGHT Detail of embossed ornament on a silver flask and the lid of a silver casket in the Esquiline Treasure, Rome, second half of 4th century AD. *British Museum*, MLA 66.12–29.4 and 2. CENTRE Bronze skillet handle with the maker's name POMP, for Pomponius. Colchester, 1st–2nd centuries AD. Length 100 mm. *British Museum*, PRB 1870.4–2.184.

76 LEFT From the workshop of Menophilos, Myrina, Turkey,

early 1st century AD. Height 275 mm. *British Museum*. RIGHT Probably made in Gaul, early 2nd century AD. Height 200 mm. *Verulamium Museum*, St Albans. BELOW Egypt, first half of 1st century AD. Height 143 mm. *Museum of Fine Arts*, Budapest.

77 ABOVE Grave 5, Köln-Braunsfeld, near Cologne, 4th century AD. Height 121 mm. Webster, L. and Brown, L. (eds.) 1997, *The Transformation of the Roman World AD 400–900*, London, pl. 46, p. 167. LEFT Junglinster, Luxemburg, 4th century AD. Height 203 mm. *Museum of History and Art*, Luxemburg. RIGHT Syria, AD 50–100. Height 208 mm. *British Museum*, Glass 1373.

78 Lead-glazed pottery. LEFT Colchester, Essex, middle of 1st century AD. Height 185 mm. *Castle Museum*, Colchester. RIGHT ABOVE Hama, Syria, 1st century BC or first century AD. Height 55 mm. *Metropolitan Museum of Art*, New York. RIGHT BELOW No provenance, Asia Minor, 1st century BC or 1st century AD. Diameter 83 mm. *British Museum*. BELOW Oswald and Pryce op. cit. (see **26–27**), pl. LII, 5, 8, 9.

79 Covered vase and plate from Egypt, perhaps Memphis. Probably 1st century BC. ABOVE Height 170 mm. *Museum für Kunst und Gewerbe*, Hamburg. BELOW Diameter 215 mm.

80 ABOVE LEFT Italy, made in the workshop of M. PEREN-NIUS BARGATHES at Arezzo, c. AD 10–15. Height 183 mm. *Metropolitan Museum of Art*, New York. BELOW RIGHT Oswald and Pryce op. cit., pl. XII, 3. Made at Lezoux, Auvergne, 2nd century AD. Height 225 mm. Outlines of Italian and provincial pottery of Arretine and Samian type, Oswald and Pryce op. cit., pls XL, 4; XLVIII, 1, 17; XXXVIII, 1.

81 ABOVE RIGHT Italy, factory of CN ATEIUS, c. 10–5 BC. Found in Mainz. *Römisch-Germanisches Zentralmuseum*, Mainz. Outlines of Italian and provincial pottery of Arretine and Samian type. Oswald and Pryce op. cit., pls II, 1; XVI, 1; XLI, 2; XLII, 4; LV, 2; LXIX, 1, 2.

82 Provincial pottery. LEFT Castor (Nene Valley) ware, late 2nd or 3rd century AD. Height 145 mm. *Royal Ontario Museum of Archaeology*, Toronto. RIGHT probably from Gaul, found at Silchester. 3rd century AD. Height 125 mm. *Reading Museum*. Outlines of provincial pottery from Oswald and Pryce op. cit., pls LXXIX, 5, 12; LXXXI, 6; LXXXII, 10.

83 Verulamium, Hertfordshire, late 2nd or early 3rd century AD. Height 230 mm. *Verulamium Museum*, St Albans.

84 ABOVE LEFT From Cologne, probably made in Rheinzabern or Trier, 3rd century AD. Height 150 mm. ABOVE RIGHT Found at Araines, probably from Lezoux, mid-2nd century AD. Height 95 mm. *Ashmolean Museum*, Oxford. BELOW LEFT From Cologne, second half of 1st century AD. Height 110 mm. *Victoria and Albert Museum*, London. BELOW RIGHT Bonn, made in the Rhineland, 2nd century AD. Height 130 mm. *Rheinisches Landesmuseum*, Bonn.

85 Colchester, Essex; buff clay with modelled design, late 2nd or early 3rd century AD. Height 26 and 27 mm. *Castle Museum*, Colchester.

86 The Esquiline Treasure, Rome, second half of 4th century AD. Design on a silver pan. Length 370 mm. *Musée du Petit Palais*, Paris.

87 ABOVE LEFT Bone hair pin. Probably made in London, 1st century AD. *British Museum*, PRB OA245. ABOVE CENTRE Gold and pearl ear-rings, 1st–2nd centuries AD. Length 22 and 23 mm. *Museum für Kunst und Gewerbe*, Hamburg. ABOVE RIGHT Portrait of a woman found with a mummy at Hawara, Egypt. 2nd century AD. *British Museum*, EA NG1269. CENTRE Centrepiece from a plaited gold necklace from Rome set with garnets. A sapphire makes up the body of the butterfly design while the wings are of a white material.

The loop at the end of the butterfly design may be a later addition. Width across the wings c. 20 mm. *British Museum*, Jewellery 3135. BELOW Tortosa, Syria, 2nd–3rd centuries AD. Herakles-knot gold links, length 15 mm. Stones emeralds. *British Museum*, Jewellery 2730.

88 ABOVE LEFT Detail from a mummy portrait from Egypt, 4th century AD. *British Museum*. ABOVE RIGHT Gold snake bracelet. Pompeii, 1st century AD. *British Museum*, GR 1946.7–2.2. CENTRE Gold snake bracelet. No provenance, 1st century BC. *Museo Archeologico Nazionale*, Naples. From *Museo Borbonico*, VII, 1831, pl. XLVI. BELOW From the jeweller's hoard, Snettisham, Norfolk, 2nd century AD. Two silver bracelets, one extended to show design. Two silver finger rings. Internal dimensions 20 × 15 mm and 20 × 17 mm. *British Museum*, PRB P.1986.4–313, 315, 244, 275.

89 LEFT ABOVE and CENTRE The Thetford Treasure, Gallows Hill, Thetford, Norfolk, late 4th century AD. Gold ring. The plait effect is produced by laying twisted wire side by side. Green glass bezel. Internal dimensions 18 × 16 mm. *British Museum*, PRB P.1981.2–15. El Fayum, Egypt, 2nd century AD. Gold chain necklace with medallion fastener. A Medusa head on the medallion. *Walters Art Gallery*, Baltimore. RIGHT ABOVE and CENTRE Silver wire ring and chain with fastener from the jeweller's hoard, Snettisham, Norfolk, 2nd century AD. Internal dimensions of the ring 16 × 17 mm. Diameter of dome 29 mm. *British Museum*, PRB P.1986.4–1.289, 327–8. BELOW Diagram showing gold chain types. From Ogden, J. 1992, *Ancient Jewellery, Interpreting the Past*, London, fig. 32 a–e.

90 LEFT Funerary relief of Tamma, daughter of Shamsigeram. Palmyra, Syria, 2nd century AD. *British Museum*, WA 105204. CENTRE Gold ear-rings with pearls and

garnet. No provenance, 1st century AD. Length 48 mm. *Antikenmuseum, Staatliche Museen Preussischer Kulturbesitz*, Berlin, 30219.428. RIGHT Gold hair ornament with emeralds (square setting), pearls and sapphire (centre drop). Said to be from Tunis, 3rd century AD. Length 108 mm. *British Museum*, Jewellery 2866. BELOW The Hoxne Treasure, Hoxne, Suffolk, late 4th–early 5th centuries AD. Extended design of pierced and engraved gold bracelet. Width c. 20 mm. *British Museum*, PRB P.1994.4–17.

91 The Thetford Treasure, Gallows Hill, Thetford, Norfolk, late 4th century AD. TOP RIGHT Gold buckle. Length of plate 52 mm. Four gold rings from the same hoard: LEFT, FROM THE TOP No.7, bezel of blue-green glass, internal dimensions 18 × 14 mm; no.10, oval gold bezel with clasped right hands, internal dimensions 18 × 15 mm; no.5, in the centre a box setting of an amethyst surrounded by eight cells with garnets in the circular and emeralds in the sub-rectangular cells (some stones are missing), internal dimensions 20 × 16 mm. BELOW RIGHT No.2, bezel is an engraved amethyst, showing cupid riding a lion, internal diameter 20 mm. *British Museum*, PRB P.1981.2–1, 7, 10, 5, 2. Drawings after Philip Compton in Johns and Potter op. cit. (see **67**).

92 Roman Britain. ABOVE LEFT and RIGHT Bronze brooches with blue, red and ?white enamel. Length c. 60 mm. *British Museum*. ABOVE CENTRE Kirkby Lathorpe. Bronze handle with blue enamel on a white bedding matrix. Length of handle 115 mm. From a photograph in the possession of English Heritage. BELOW LEFT Nornour, Isles of Scilly. Wheel brooch in bronze with green enamel in the outer spokes, millefiore in blue, white and red round the rim and blue enamel in the centre. Diameter c. 55 mm. Dudley, D. and Hull, M.R. 1968, 'Excavations at Nornour in the Isles of Scilly',

Archaeological Journal, 124, no. 205. After a drawing by D.S. Neal. BELOW RIGHT Bronze pendant with blue, green and orange enamel. Castor, Northants. Width c. 40 mm. *British Museum*, PRB 1909.6–7.1. All 2nd century AD.

93 ABOVE LEFT Kingsholm, Gloucestershire, 2nd century AD. Bronze brooch with enamel inlay in two colours, one identified as red. Length 67 mm. ABOVE RIGHT The Backworth Treasure, Northumberland, c. AD 140. Silver-gilt brooch. Length 105 mm. BELOW LEFT St Paul's, Lincoln, late 3rd or 4th century AD. Length 67 mm. BELOW RIGHT Moray Firth, Scotland, 4th century AD. Gold brooch with niello inlay. Length 79 mm. All *British Museum*.

94 The Fulham sword, from the River Thames at Fulham, first half of the 1st century AD. LEFT The design on the scabbard, based on a drawing by Nick Griffiths, 1995. *British Museum*, PRB 1883.4–7.1. CENTRE Reconstruction of the sword and scabbard. RIGHT Tombstone of Roman centurion from near Beverley Road, Colchester, AD 43–60. *Castle Museum*, Colchester.

95 Bronze tinned or silvered belt mounts, 1st century AD. After Grew, F. and Griffiths, N. 1991, 'The pre-Flavian military belt: the evidence from Britain', *Archaeologia*, 109, 46–84. ABOVE No.3, Hod Hill, Dorset. LEFT ABOVE No.154, Hod Hill, Dorset. LEFT CENTRE No.67, Colchester, Essex. LEFT BELOW No.1, Colchester, Essex. RIGHT ABOVE No.72, Richborough, Kent. RIGHT CENTRE No.66, Chichester, Sussex. RIGHT BELOW No.5, Colchester, Essex.

96 ABOVE Made in Italy, late 2nd or early 3rd century AD. 147 × 96 mm. BELOW Made in Italy 15 BC–AD 15. Said to be from Pozzuoli. 104 × 72 mm. *British Museum*, Q1349, Q761.

97 Two views of an earthenware pot with slightly burnished, dark surface and decoration in relief. Grave find from West Lodge, Colchester, Essex, AD 175. Height 215 mm.

98 ABOVE LEFT Hontheim-an-der-Mosel, Rheinland-Pfalz, Germany, late 4th–early 5th centuries AD. Belt buckle, bronze. Width 123 mm. *Rheinisches Landesmuseum*, Bonn. BELOW LEFT Enns (Roman *Lauriacum*), Austria, late

4th–early 5th centuries AD. Belt mount, bronze. Length 78 mm. *Enns Museum*. ABOVE RIGHT Aquileia, Friuli, Italy, late 4th century AD. *Aquileia Museum*. BELOW RIGHT Furfooz, Namur, Belgium, late 4th century AD. Strap-end, bronze. *Namur Museum*.

99 ABOVE Enns, Austria, late 4th–early 5th centuries AD. Belt

mount, bronze. Length 113 mm. *Enns Museum*. BELOW Reconstruction of use after Bullinger, H. 1969, *Spätantike Gürtelbeschläge. Typen, Herstellung, Trageweise und Datierung*, Dissertationes Archaeologicae Gandenses 12, Abb. 21.2.

100 Pompeii, Italy, 1st century AD. ABOVE House of P.

Proculus. This is a sketch, not a measured drawing. BELOW *Museo Nazionale*, Naples.

Further reading

Burn, L. *The British Museum Book of Greek and Roman Art*, London 1991.

Field, R. *Geometric Patterns from Roman Mosaics*, Diss 1988.

Fletcher, Sir Banister *A History of Architecture on the Comparative Method for Students, Craftsmen and Amateurs*, London 1931, first published 1896.

Gombrich, E.H. *The Sense of Order, A Study of the Psychology of Decorative Art*, 2nd edn, Oxford 1984.

Green, K. *Roman Pottery. Interpreting the Past*, London 1992.

Jenkins, I. *Greek and Roman Life*, London 1986.

Johnson, P. *Romano-British Mosaics*, Shire Archaeology 25, Aylesbury 1987.

Ling, R. *Romano-British Wallpainting*, Shire Archaeology 42, Aylesbury 1985.

Ling, R. *Ancient Mosaics*, London 1998.

Potter, T.W. *Roman Britain*, 2nd edn, London 1997.

Tomlinson, A.R. *Greek and Roman Architecture*, London 1995.

Walker, S. *Roman Art*, London 1991.

Walker, S. *Greek and Roman Portraits*, London 1995.

Wilson, E. *8000 Years of Ornament. An Illustrated Handbook of Motifs*, London 1994.

1 A Roman celebration of decoration. Bronze pan handle, inlaid with copper and black niello, from Prickwillow, Isle of Ely, signed BODUOGENUS. The name is Celtic; the artist may have been British or French, but the ornament is totally Mediterranean. 2nd century AD.

2 The rich variety of motifs in Roman decoration was the result of the long history of decorative art in the Mediterranean. Plaques and openwork crests of fired clay (terracotta) protected wooden structures in the early temple buildings in west central Italy. Examples from the 6th century BC onwards.

3 These simple designs remained popular for centuries. The design of the open-work crest ABOVE occurs on many sites in the 3rd and 2nd centuries BC. The design from the 6th–5th centuries BC on a plaque BELOW, is an elaborate example of the lotus-and-palmette border motif (see **4–5**).

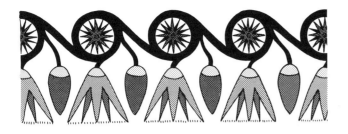 

4 ABOVE The border of lotus flowers and buds first appears in Egypt in the second millennium BC (p. 10). CENTRE On Greek pottery the palmette often takes the place of the bud in the design. BELOW AND **5** Contemporary terracotta temple decorations in west central Italy make use of the motif with many variations.

5 Lotus-and-palmette border designs on terracotta plaques from west central Italy from the late 6th and 5th centuries BC. The designs are picked out in white, red and black on a cream slip.

6 The palmette motif was one of several motifs which appeared in Greece in the late 8th century BC (p. 10). ABOVE Painted on pottery from Rhodes *c.* 650, and CENTRE LEFT and RIGHT on pottery from Athens and the Greek colony at Apulia, Italy, late 6th–4th centuries BC. BELOW Painted on terracotta tiles in red and black on a cream ground. From the temple at the Belvedere, Orvieto. Early 5th century BC.

7 The diagonal placing of the palmettes is typical of the design in Italy BELOW, OPPOSITE and ABOVE. Moulded terracotta plaques, ABOVE from Latium (Lazio), 400–300 BC; BELOW from Alatri, Etruria (Tuscany), late 3rd or 2nd centuries BC.

8 The lotus-and-palmette borders are sometimes inhabited by nymphs and fauns. ABOVE Engraved in bronze on a vessel from the second half of the 4th century BC; CENTRE and BELOW on moulded terracotta plaques from the 2nd century BC–1st century AD.

9 Palmette and spiral designs, developing plant-like forms, are particularly common in architectural ornament. ABOVE LEFT Terracotta plaque from the Temple of Juno Sospita in Lanuvium (Lazio), 1st century BC. ABOVE RIGHT Stone carving at Palmyra, Syria, early 3rd century AD, and BELOW at the Temple of Apollo at Didyma, Anatolia (Turkey), 1st century AD.

10 Examples of the Doric LEFT and Ionic CENTRE and RIGHT Orders of classical architecture. These are formalised versions of the basic post-and-lintel (column and entablature) structure, each having its own rules for design and proportion (p. 10). LEFT and CENTRE Athens, Greece, 5th century BC; RIGHT Rome, 100 BC.

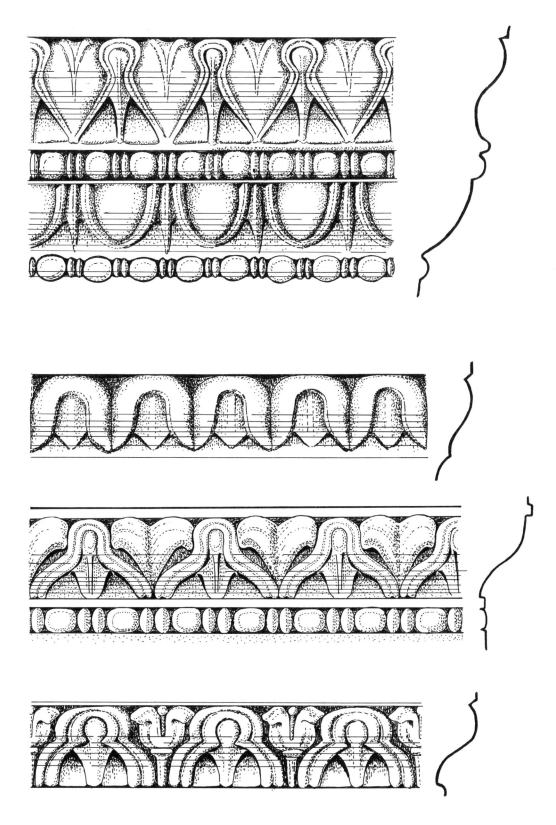

11 ABOVE Example of mouldings used in the Greek Ionic Order. A leaf-and-dart (also known as waterleaf) motif on the *cyma reversa* (the double curved section of the moulding) is followed by bead-and-reel motifs on either side of the egg-and-dart motif on the *ovolo* (also known as *astragal*, a convex moulding). Athens, late 5th century BC. BELOW Three variations on these motifs in Roman architecture from Pompeii, Palmyra in Syria and Rome, 1st–2nd centuries AD.

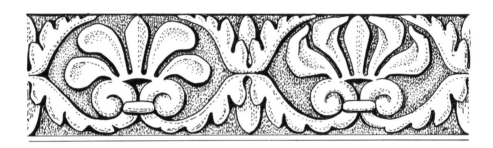

12 ABOVE Frieze from the Greek Ionic Order. Basically a lotus-and-palmette design with acanthus leaves added, this motif is commonly known as *anthemion* (honeysuckle). Athens, late 5th century BC. BELOW Roman variations on frieze designs from Rome and Jerash in Syria, 1st–2nd centuries AD.

13 LEFT Example of the Greek Corinthian Order. Athens, 335 BC. TOP CENTRE A variation on the Corinthian capital. Athens, 100–35 BC. RIGHT and CENTRE Example of the Roman Corinthian Order and a pilaster capital from the Pantheon, Rome, 2nd century AD. BELOW, Corinthian capital from the Temple of Castor and Pollux. Rome, 1st century AD.

14 The motif known as 'acanthus' has been associated with the commonly occur-ring plants *Acanthus spinosus* and *Acanthus mollis* (ABOVE and p. 10). CENTRE In the art of classical Greece the motif was added to the palmette, creating apparently realistic plant forms. Athens, *c*. 390–365 BC. BELOW In Roman art the acanthus leaf scroll became very popular. Aphrodisias, Turkey, *c*. AD 200.

15 A detail from an elaborate acanthus scroll which decorates marble panels on the *Ara Pacis Augustae* in Rome, dedicated in AD 9. This form of the motif was regarded as an ideal at the time and is still used in decoration today.

16 On a terracotta plaque Victory, in the shape of a winged figure, stands on an acanthus plant in the style of the *Ara Pacis*, an imperial motif used here for domestic purposes. Rome, 30 BC–AD 20. BELOW Acanthus scrolls and winged figures from the base of a lamp-stand. Probably 1st century AD.

17 LEFT A common decorative motif is known as 'candelabra'. It depicts flames rising from an elaborate arrangement of flowers and vases. Carved in low relief on a marble pilaster, AD 1–50. RIGHT Cupids bearing the armour of Mars decorate three sides of a lamp-stand base in low relief. Probably 1st century AD. See also **60–62**.

18 The acanthus scroll, with or without additional real or imaginary flowers, is a common motif in all parts of the Roman world. ABOVE Two floral acanthus scroll borders from Palmyra, Syria, 1st century and first half of 3rd century AD. BELOW Stylised leaf scrolls in mosaic from Roman Britain, 4th century AD.

19 ABOVE LEFT and RIGHT Acanthus scrolls and flower in mosaic from Roman Carthage, North Africa, 4th century AD. BELOW LEFT An acanthus flower in mosaic from Roman Britain, 3rd century AD.

20 The decorative use of the ivy leaf is associated with the popular cult of Bacchus. ABOVE Ivy design from a Greek vase in Italy, 370–360 BC. CENTRE Stylised ivy designs engraved on silver from the early 2nd century AD. BELOW and OPPOSITE LEFT Leaf designs in mosaic from Roman Britain in the 4th century AD.

21 Realistic and formalised leaves set within winding stems or bands. ABOVE LEFT Roman Britain; ABOVE RIGHT Palmyra; BELOW Roman Carthage. 1st–5th centuries AD.

22 Garlands carved in marble on a child's sarcophagus from Libya. Made in Italy, AD 120–40.

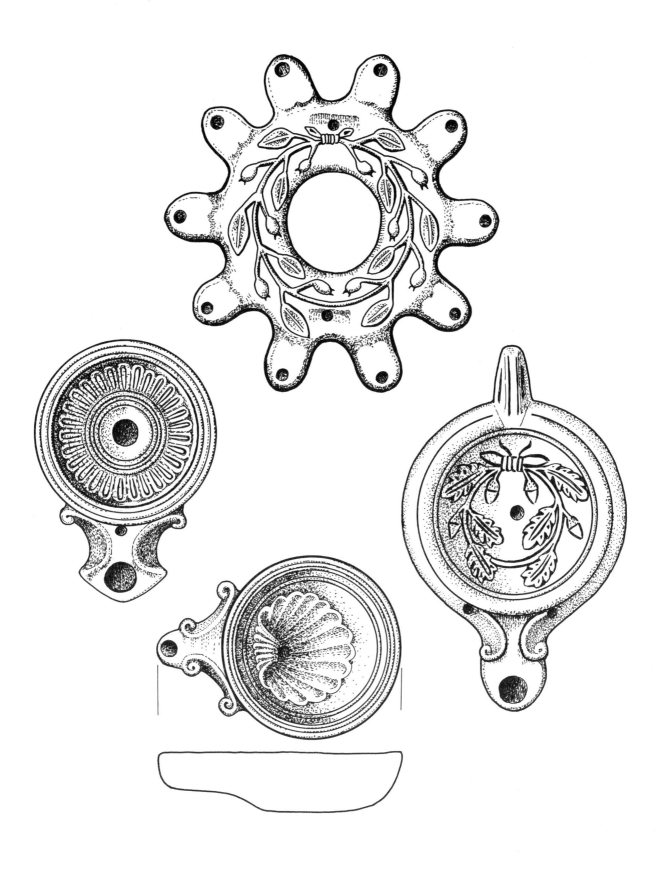

23 Clay lamps made in Italy. 1st century AD.

24 The vine scroll was associated with the Bacchus cult. RIGHT and TOP OPPOSITE Carved borders from Palmyra, Syria, 1st–2nd centuries AD. BELOW Vine leaves engraved in silver from Hoxne, Suffolk, late 4th–early 5th centuries AD. The vine scroll continued as a motif in Christian art. LEFT and CENTRE Tapestry band and roundel from Christian Coptic Egypt, 4th–5th centuries AD.

25 The vine scroll motif – and the drinking of wine – reached all parts of the Empire and beyond. These examples are from the 1st–3rd centuries AD and FROM THE TOP come from Palmyra, Syria; Gandhara, Afghanistan; Colchester, Essex; and Sidon, Lebanon.

26–27 Leaf scroll motifs from provincial Roman red-slip pottery. 1st century AD. TOP A cup from Sandy, Bedfordshire, made in La Graufesenque, France, c. AD 50.

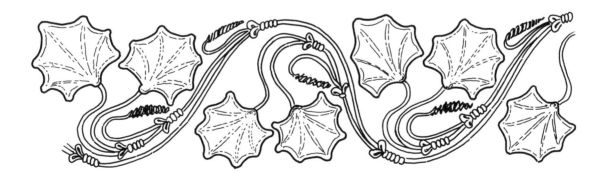

28 The linked spirals known as running dog or wave scroll and the meander are curved and angular variations on the same motif. In the same way the four-strand spiral and the swastika are closely related motifs (p. 12). The combination of the meander and the swastika as borders or area-filling designs is very common in Roman decorative art (**44, 46**).

29 Wave scroll and meander motifs, 1st–2nd centuries AD. From mosaic pavements and BELOW painted and shaded to imitate a stone frieze in Pompeii.

30 The Labyrinth in the story of Theseus and the Minotaur can be represented by a meander pattern (named after the river in Anatolia where the design occurs on coins, ABOVE LEFT) as shown on a Greek bowl, ABOVE RIGHT. The Labyrinth can also be represented by a maze, shown here on a coin from Crete ABOVE LEFT and BELOW on a mosaic from Pompeii (p. 12).

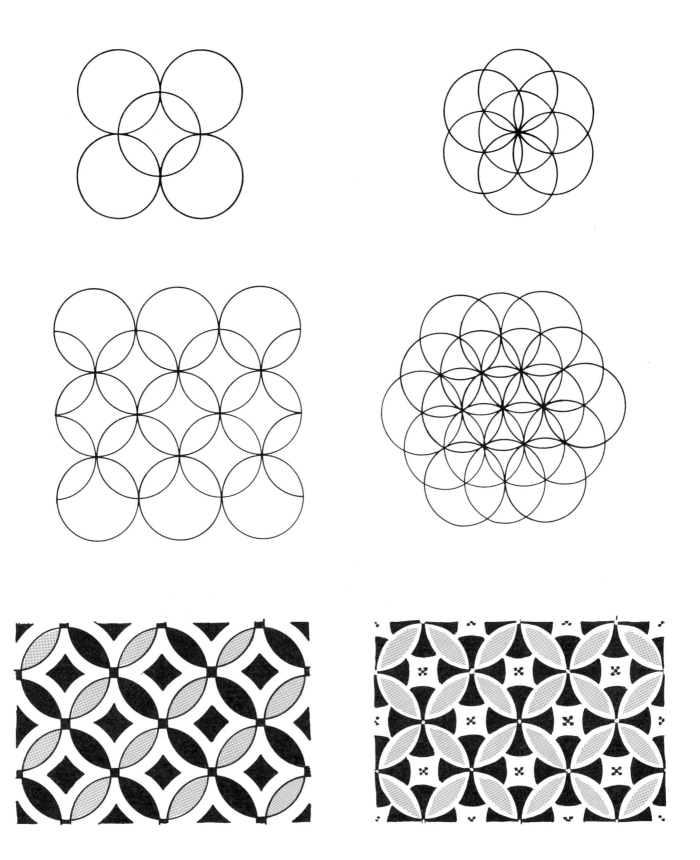

31 Intersecting circles are the basis for a large number of designs. These simple constructions can be used as grids on which designs are drawn (**32–34**) or patterns produced by applying colour to different parts. BELOW Mosaic designs from Antioch, Turkey, 2nd century AD.

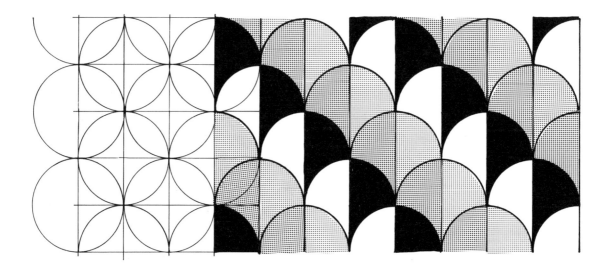

32 Two popular designs based on a grid of intersecting circles. While the design ABOVE comes from a mosaic pavement in Britain from the 3rd century AD and that BELOW from a pillar at Pompeii from the 1st century AD, they can be found almost everywhere and at all times in the Roman Empire.

33 The pelta motif (named after a small shield used by the Amazons in Greek mythology) is best drawn on a grid of intersecting circles. This is a common motif on mosaic pavements in Roman Britain. Another version of the motif is illustrated BELOW.

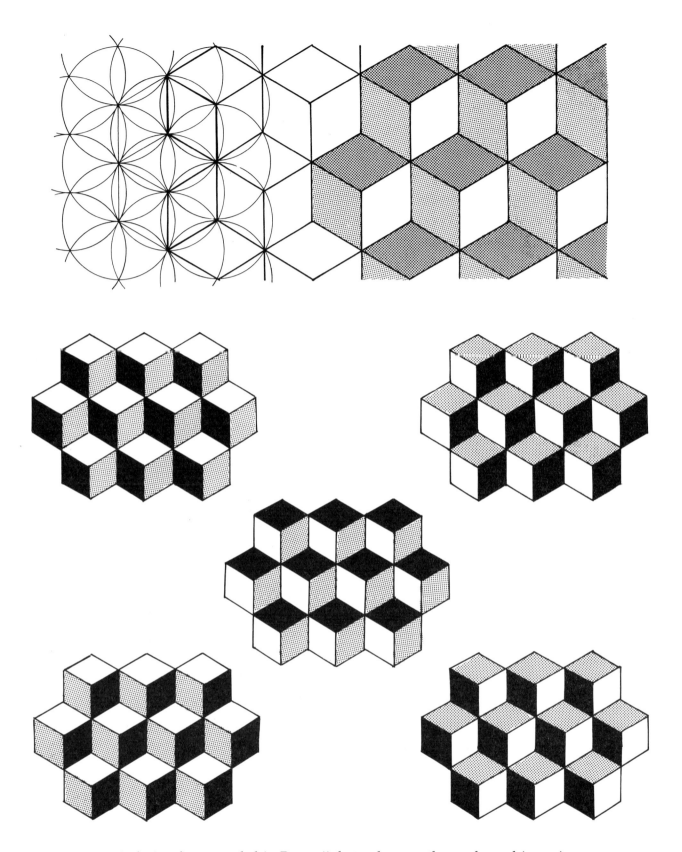

34 A design first recorded in Pompeii, but subsequently much used in various mosaic techniques. It is made up of identical lozenges in three colours to create designs which appear as sets of three-dimensional cubes. ABOVE The design and its construction from hexagons. BELOW By altering the viewpoint, and reversing the white and medium-coloured lozenges relative to the black, different effects are created.

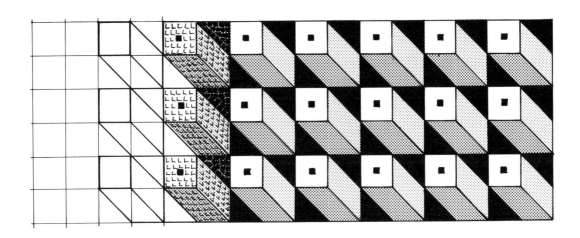

35 A three-dimensional effect is frequently achieved in mosaic pavements. In many instances these appear to imitate architectural features. They are not, however, isometric projections, nor do they represent true perspective (p. 13).

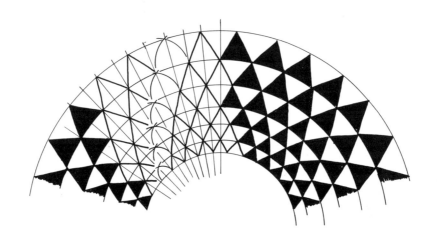

36 Roundels in the Blackfriar's Pavement in Leicester (*c.* AD 150) ABOVE show the popular 'shield' motif. The method used here distorts the shape of the triangles and is not the one used elsewhere when the motif is very large. A construction which allows the triangles to remain equilateral in all bands is indicated BELOW.

37 Other roundels on the Blackfriar's Pavement in Leicester have designs which could be constructed on a grid of intersecting circles. The border design BELOW comes from the same pavement.

38 The so-called Solomon's Knot, which is not a knot, and its variations are common motifs in mosaic pavement designs.

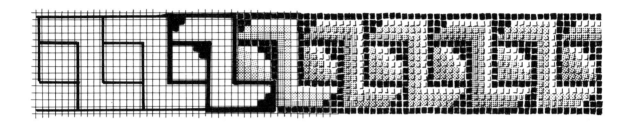

39 Like the knots in **38**, twists and plaits are motifs which are based on geometric construction and do not as a rule portray real plaits in a functional capacity. Appropriately shaded they do, however, produce a three-dimensional effect.

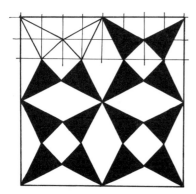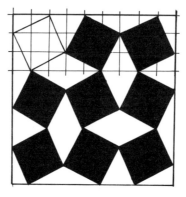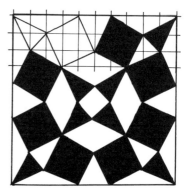

40 ABOVE Detail of the design of one of the earliest black and white mosaic pavements in Britain, from Fishbourne, Sussex, with a suggested grid of construction. The design is confusing, because of the apparently random positioning of the small lozenge-shaped elements. The sophisticated arrangement of patterns in the squares from another mosaic at Fishbourne, the grids divided into 8, 9 and 10 parts respectively BELOW, would suggest that this effect is deliberate. About AD 75–80.

41 The design on a mosaic pavement from North Hill, Colchester, is based on octagons, producing a central panel and stars constructed of lozenges between square and rectangular panels. The central motif is detailed BELOW LEFT and one octagon motif BELOW RIGHT. The lozenge shapes which form the stars can also be seen as the sides of a box. Colours are black and white with a little red and yellow in the floral motifs. Second half of 2nd century AD.

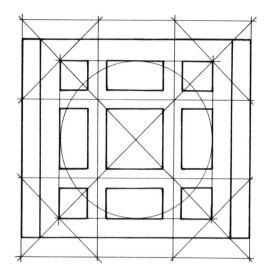

42 Mosaic pavement from Verulamium, Hertfordshire, 2nd century AD. ABOVE A suggested grid on which it could have been constructed.

43 Details of the central 'dahlia' design and corner rosettes in **42**. These motifs are outlined in black, with red and yellow detail, on a light-coloured ground.

44 Mosaic pavement from Verulamium, Hertfordshire. The swastika meander border creates fields filled with cups and flowers, together with a central panel. The bands in the plait design are made up of five rows of tesserae – black, red, yellow, white and black. 2nd century AD.

45 The pavement in **44** is known as the 'Cernunnus' mosaic, referring to a suggestion that the figure in the centre is the Celtic god of that name, who was often shown with a horned head. He is, however, more likely to be Oceanus, a Roman deity, with lobster claws on his head.

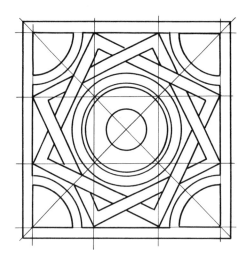

46–47 Mosaic pavement from Kingscote, Gloucestershire. **46** ABOVE A grid showing how this design could have been constructed. The fine Venus figure and wreath in the centre are unfortunately damaged. **47** Other details from the design. Late 3rd or early 4th century AD.

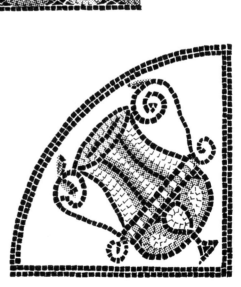

48 Examples of the vine cup motif (*cantharus*) from different mosaics in Roman Britain. This motif was associated with the popular wine-drinking cult of Bacchus. BELOW Peacocks on either side of a vase form a common motif sometimes symbolising immortality (see **64**).

49 The central roundel in the large mosaic floor from Hinton St Mary in Dorset
is believed to represent Christ; if so, it is the first such representation in Britain.
Behind the head is the *chi-rho* monogram. Two pomegranates, symbols of immortality, complete the design. First half of 4th century AD.

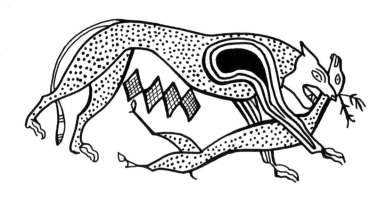

50 Three motif groups with a long history: fantastic creatures, the hunt and scenes from mythology are well represented in Roman decoration. ABOVE From a Mesopotamian cylinder seal, 3rd millennium BC. CENTRE A combat scene on a Cycladic jug, 7th century BC. BELOW A Greek plaque with a scene from the story of Bellerophon, 5th century BC.

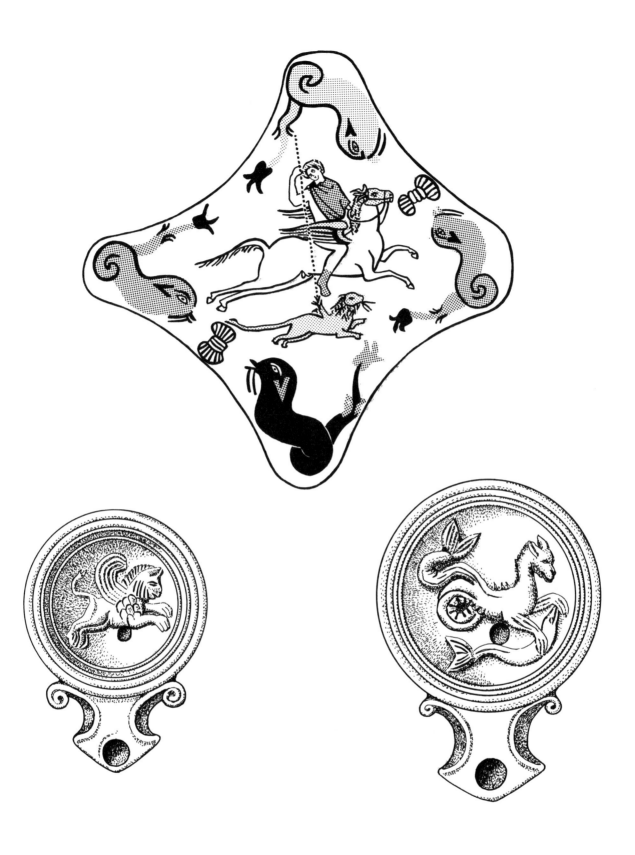

51 ABOVE In a British version in mosaic, Bellerophon, surrounded by dolphins
kills the chimera, a fire-breathing, lion-headed monster. Mid-4th century AD.
BELOW Italian clay lamps decorated with creatures made up of different animal
parts – a winged lion and a sea-horse. First third of 1st century AD.

52 The hunt celebrates an activity universally popular with the mighty as well as with the common man. ABOVE A moulded decoration on pottery from the 2nd century AD. BELOW The animals in a frieze on a fragmentary silver bowl in the Traprain Treasure, Scotland, can be identified so clearly as particular species that the maker is likely to have known them by sight. Early 5th century AD.

53 A hoard from Mildenhall, Suffolk, included a silver bowl with a hunting frieze round the rim. The head in the centre may represent Alexander the Great. 4th century AD.

54 A mosaic at Fishbourne Roman Palace, Sussex, has Cupid riding on a dolphin as its central motif. Sea monsters are also part of the design. While the hippocamp is all in black, the other motifs have black outlines with shading in red and yellow on a cream ground. About AD 160.

55 A mosaic at Cirencester, Gloucestershire, has the head of a sea god (perhaps Oceanus) and sea monsters and dolphins among its motifs. In this mosaic a subtle grey shading is added in the beard to the usual colour scheme of black, red and yellow. 2nd century AD.

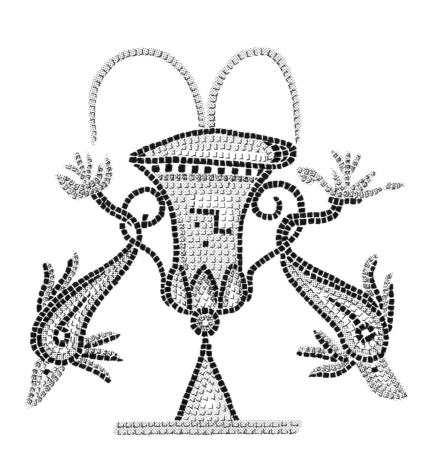

56 Playful dolphins figure in many mosaics, and suggest the sea gods by their presence. ABOVE From Verulamium, Hertfordshire, 2nd century AD. BELOW From Roman Carthage, North Africa, second half of 4th century AD.

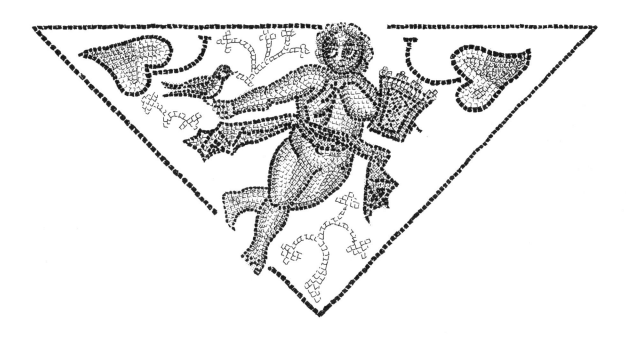

57 Figures representing the seasons are often placed in the corners of mosaic designs. In Chedworth Roman Villa, Gloucestershire, two of these remain. 'Spring' BELOW is a lightly clad girl of classical form, while 'Winter' is more realistically fitted out for British weather and is carrying a hare. 4th century AD.

58–59 Mosaic motifs from Halicarnassos, Turkey, 4th century AD. 58 The face ABOVE represents Phobos, fear personified, with BELOW a tragic mask and an image of Dionysus. 59 An observant and delightful naturalism is also part of this art.

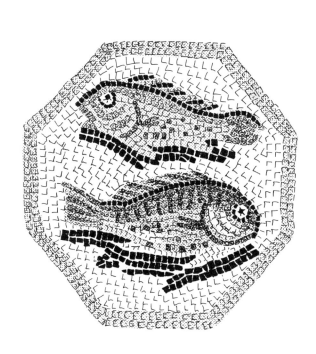

60 ABOVE On a fired clay antefix (the terminal of a roof ridge), a winged Victory carrying trophies of armour stands on a globe flanked by capricorns, the Emperor Augustus' birth sign. BELOW Decorating clay lamps from Italy are Jupiter with his eagle and thunderbolt, and Victory with palm branch and shield. 1st century AD.

61 Clay lamps. ABOVE By the lamp-maker AUGENDUS. The scene probably shows the harbour at Carthage, Tunisia. About AD 200. BELOW LEFT Probably from Italy. RIGHT From Carthage.

62 A bronze lamp-stand with a lamp soldered to the top. This has the head of Jupiter/Ammon on the handle. The flickering flame would have enhanced his grim features. Pompeii, second half of 1st century AD.

63 The stone face of the Gorgon is the centrepiece of the pediment of the Temple to Sulis Minerva in Bath. It is unusual for the Gorgon to be male, and the Celtic cast of his features suggests that the carver came from Gaul (France). 1st century AD.

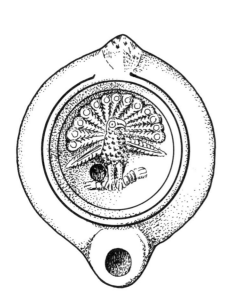
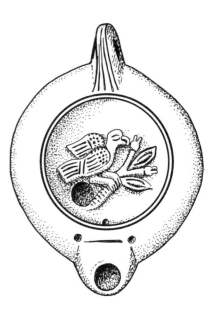

64 Birds are favourite motifs in decorative art at all times, and sometimes carry a symbolic message. The peacocks on either side of a vase carved on a tomb-chest may symbolise immortality. On a lamp the bird may be a purely decorative motif. Designs in marble relief and on clay lamps, 1st and 2nd centuries AD.

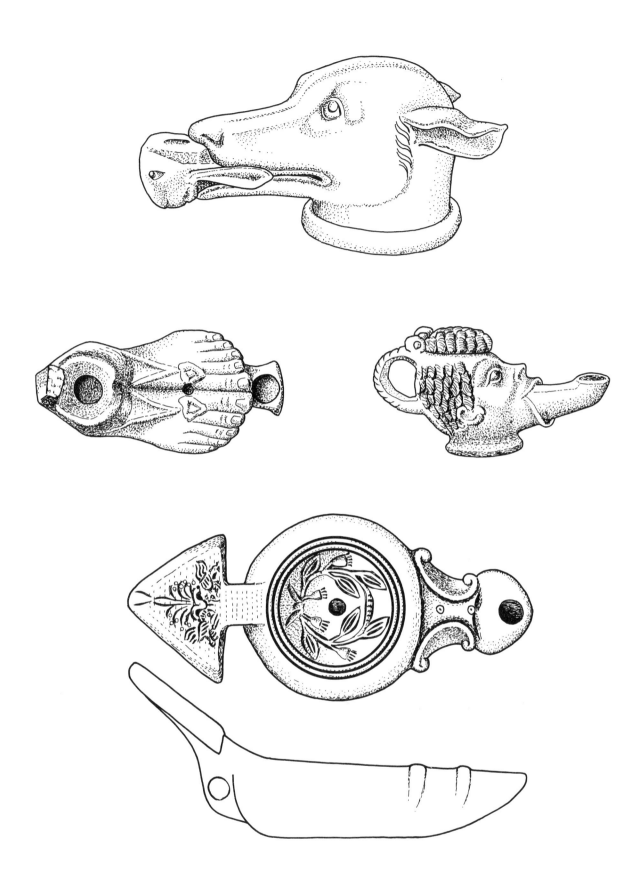

65 Italian lamps of bronze ABOVE and CENTRE RIGHT, and clay CENTRE LEFT and BELOW. 1st century AD.

66 The head of Oceanus or Neptune decorates the centre of the Great Dish from the Mildenhall Treasure, Suffolk. 4th century AD.

67 Silver-gilt spoons and strainer continue the theme associated with the sea and sea monsters. From hoards found in Britain of the 4th and early 5th centuries AD.

68 A Nereid rides a sea monster in the centre of an engraved silver bowl from the Traprain Treasure, Scotland. Late 4th–early 5th centuries AD.

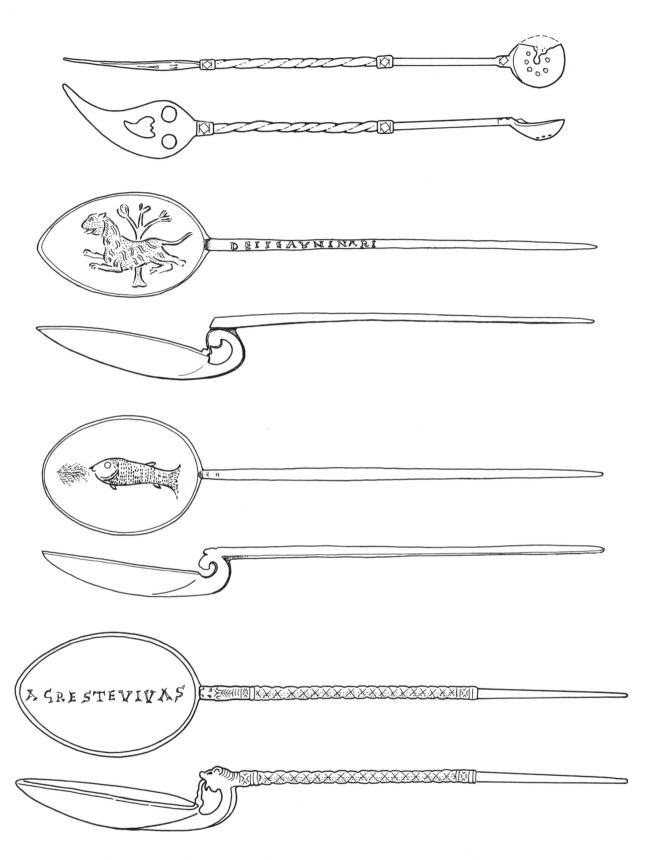

69 Three out of thirty-three silver spoons from a hoard of jewellery and silver from Thetford, Norfolk. The inscription DEIIFAVNINARI addresses Faunus, a Roman god (the spelling of DEI with two Is is a mistake). The spoons and the pick, probably a tooth-pick, would have been used at cult feasts (p. 18). Late 4th century AD.

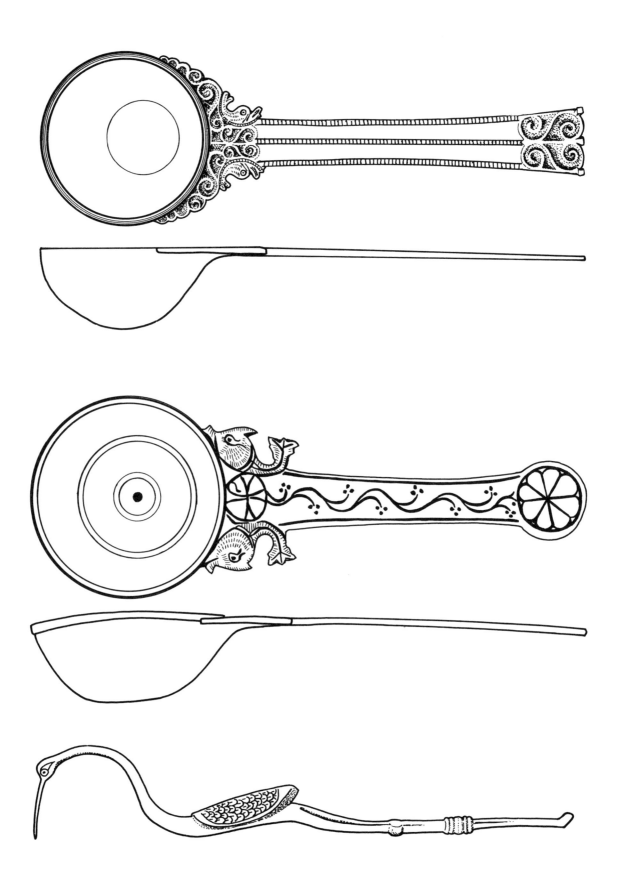

70 In the hoard from Hoxne, Suffolk, there were two sets of ten ladles. One from each set is illustrated here. The ladle ABOVE is gilded; the ladle CENTRE has the *chi-rho* monogram as part of the decoration. The implement below is a tooth- and ear-pick. Late 4th–early 5th centuries AD.

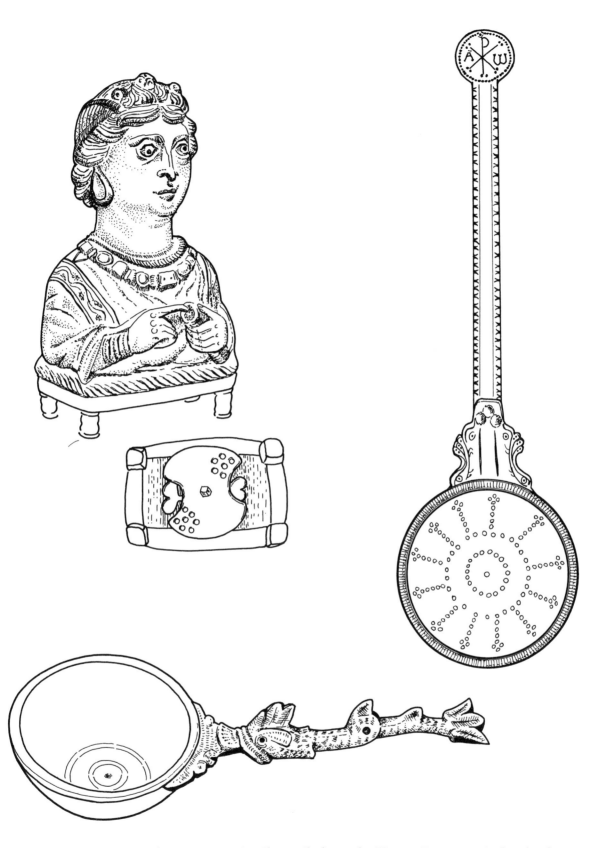

71 ABOVE LEFT A pepper pot in silver-gilt from the Hoxne Treasure. A sketch of the base shows the revolving plate and holes for sprinkling. The strainer RIGHT with the *chi-rho* and *alpha-omega* monogram is from the Water Newton hoard, Huntingdonshire, while the ladle with the dolphin handle (from a set of five) is from Mildenhall, Suffolk. 4th and early 5th centuries AD.

72 Stamped and incised patterns, inlaid with niello, on silver vessels in the Treasure from Traprain Law, Scotland. Late 4th or early 5th centuries AD.

73 Stamped and incised patterns, filled with black niello, decorate a large dish from the Mildenhall Treasure, Suffolk. A small number of stamps are used to create a variety of patterns. 4th century AD.

74 The design on a silver platter from the Mildenhall Treasure, Suffolk. A satyr and maenad are dancing to her tambourine against a background of objects associated with the cult of Bacchus. 4th century AD.

75 The scroll inhabited by figures and animals is an important decorative motif which continued in use long after the end of the Roman Empire. Here it is executed in silver LEFT and RIGHT, and in a simpler form on a bronze handle CENTRE.

76 Three goddesses. LEFT In the Hellenistic tradition of terracotta figures from Myrina, Turkey. RIGHT A bronze Venus from Verulamium, Hertfordshire, probably made in Gaul. BELOW A clay lamp from Egypt. This is a goddess for all seasons, wearing wreaths of vine leaves, grapes and lotus, as well as the crown of Isis – the sun disc between cow horns. 1st–2nd centuries AD.

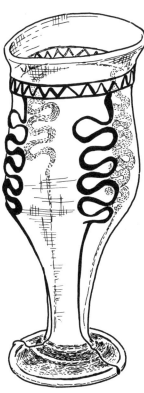

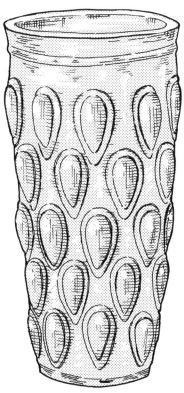

77 ABOVE Known as a cage-cup, this beaker has a fine, almost free-standing fret-work surrounding the cup, joined to the body by small pillars. Cut from a thick blank, the outer layer was coloured and changes from purple to green and yellow. The Greek letters spell 'Drink and live happily ever after'. The beaker with trailed decoration BELOW LEFT was also made in the Cologne area in the 4th century AD. BELOW RIGHT A green glass, blown in a mould, from Syria. 1st century AD.

78 Lead-glazed pottery can imitate silverware in both shape and decoration. The shapes BELOW demonstrate that Roman red-slipped ware can also have shapes and decoration which were originally created in metal. See also **80–81**.

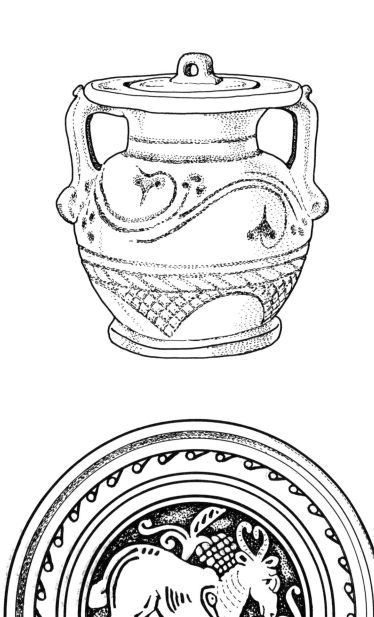

79 The design on the covered pot ABOVE was cut into the soft clay body and stands out as a darker shade of the transparent turquoise frit glaze which gathered in the grooves of the design during firing. The design on the plate BELOW is painted in manganese brown and turquoise. Note the ancient device of indicating the animal's heart. Egypt, 1st century BC.

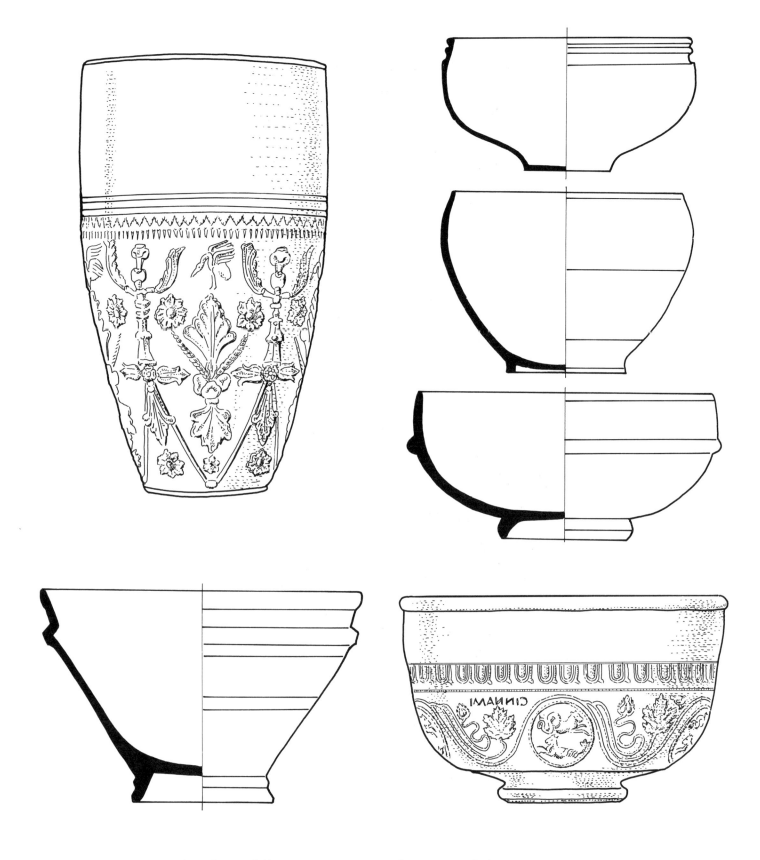

80–81 Arretine and Samian pottery uses silver-inspired decoration which could even come from moulds taken straight from contemporary silver vessels. Many skilfully potted shapes used for this type of decoration were also inspired by vessels in silver.

82 The trailing slip method of decoration known as 'barbotine' was produced by squeezing soft clay through a nozzle onto the surface of a pot. British and provincial potters used softer and rounder shapes for this kind of decoration.

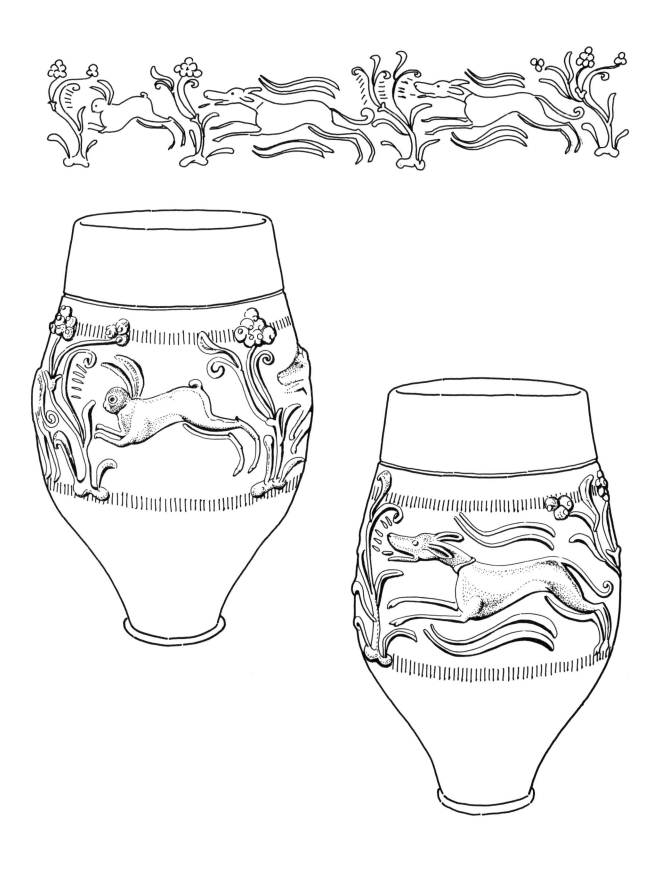

83 The trailing slip technique at its best produces very attractive results. A large beaker with a slightly burnished brown surface and a design of hare and hounds was made in the village of Castor in the Nene Valley, near Peterborough. Late 2nd or early 3rd century AD.

84 Pottery was decorated to imitate vessels in other media. ABOVE Cut and engraved glass can be identified as the source of these sharp designs, while BELOW a more sculptural application of clay appears more natural to the medium.

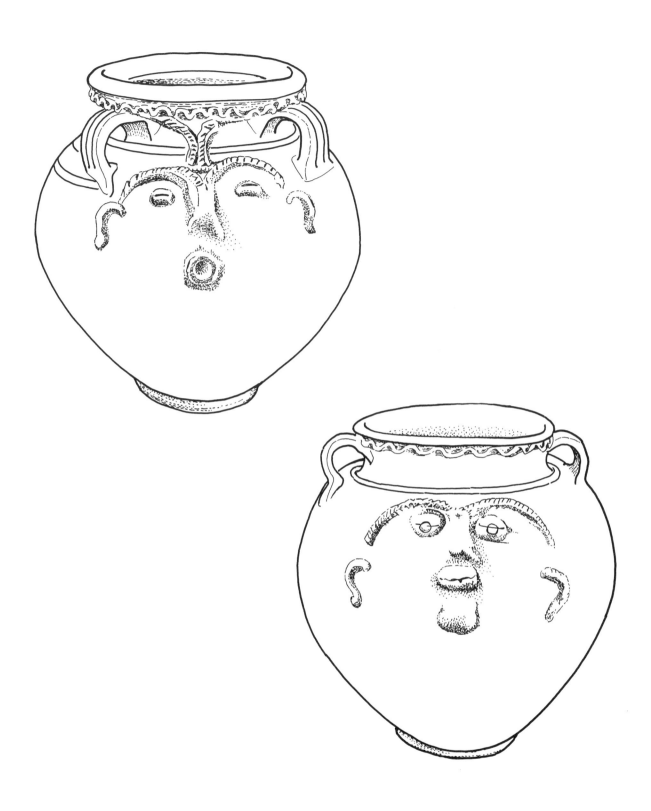

85 Coarse face-urns were often used to bury the ashes of the dead. Made in Colchester, Essex, 2nd or early 3rd century AD.

86 A silver pan in the Esquiline Treasure is fluted to emulate the inside of a shell. In the centre Venus sits dressing her hair, while one Cupid holds a mirror and the other offers a pomegranate, symbol of eternal life. On the handle are Adonis and his dog. The Treasure included a casket for cosmetics; it highlights the opulence of Roman life. 4th century AD.

87 In Egypt portraits were sometimes placed with the mummies of the dead. In Roman times these also show how jewellery was worn. Examples of jewellery shown here: a bone hair pin, pearl ear-rings, a necklace with garnets and sapphires and a butterfly pendant, and a necklace with links of Herakles-knots in gold and emeralds.

88 TOP LEFT A detail from a mummy portrait shows a snake bracelet and ring as worn. Snake jewellery was widespread in the Roman world. The gold bracelets TOP RIGHT and CENTRE are from Pompeii, while BELOW very simple silver versions for the local British market are from the jeweller's hoard at Snettisham. 2nd century AD. One bracelet is shown here extended.

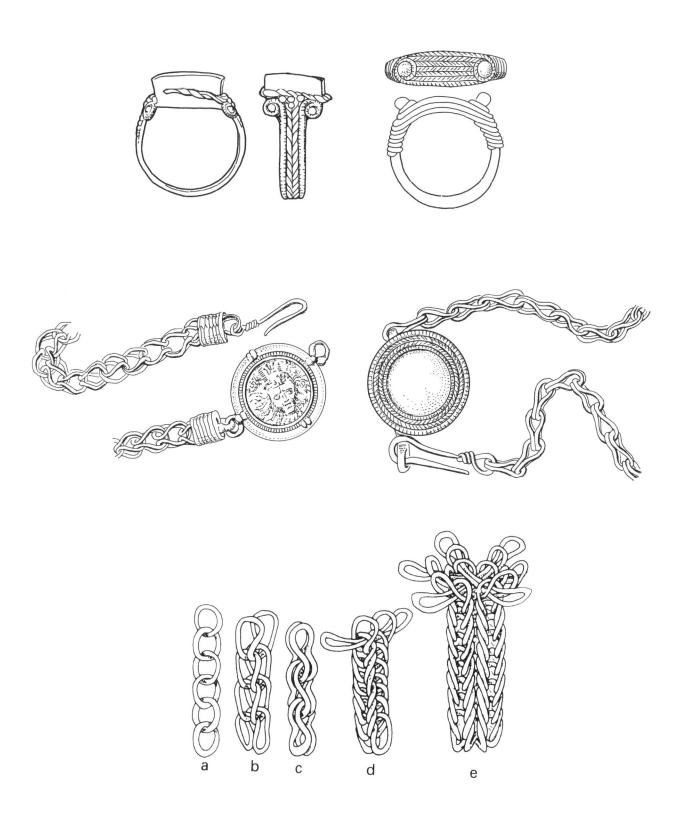

89 Much jewellery was made of wire, twisted and applied as decoration, or fashioned into links to make chains. BELOW (a) a simple or plain chain; (b) the basic loop-in-loop chain; (c) figure-eight loop-in-loop chain; (d) doubled loop-in-loop chain; (e) three-fold doubled loop-in-loop chain (from Ogden, J., 1992, *Ancient Jewellery, Interpreting the Past*, London, fig. 32).

90 A funerary relief in Palmyra, Syria, portrays Tamma, daughter of Shamsi-geram, wearing much jewellery and holding a spindle. Some of the patterns on her dress are also indicated. 2nd century AD. TOP CENTRE and RIGHT Ear-rings and hair ornament of gold with pearls, sapphires and emeralds. BELOW The extended design of a pierced and engraved gold bracelet from the Hoxne Treasure, Suffolk. Late 4th–early 5th centuries AD.

91 Some of the gold jewellery in the Thetford Treasure, Norfolk, from the late 4th century AD. The buckle has a representation of a satyr and a bunch of grapes. The rings are of a variety of styles. Woodpeckers support a caged glass bezel on one, while the bezel of the other has two clasped hands. Dolphins support a bezel set with an amethyst, emeralds and garnets, and an engraved amethyst is set in a ring with leaf designs on the band.

92 Enamelling was much used in Celtic jewellery in Britain and Gaul. The bronze 'dragon-brooches' TOP LEFT and RIGHT show traces of Celtic elements in the design. The enamel in these, and in the pan handle CENTRE, is mostly red and blue. In the bronze brooch and pendant BELOW other colours, including green and orange, also occur, as well as some millefiori. 2nd century AD.

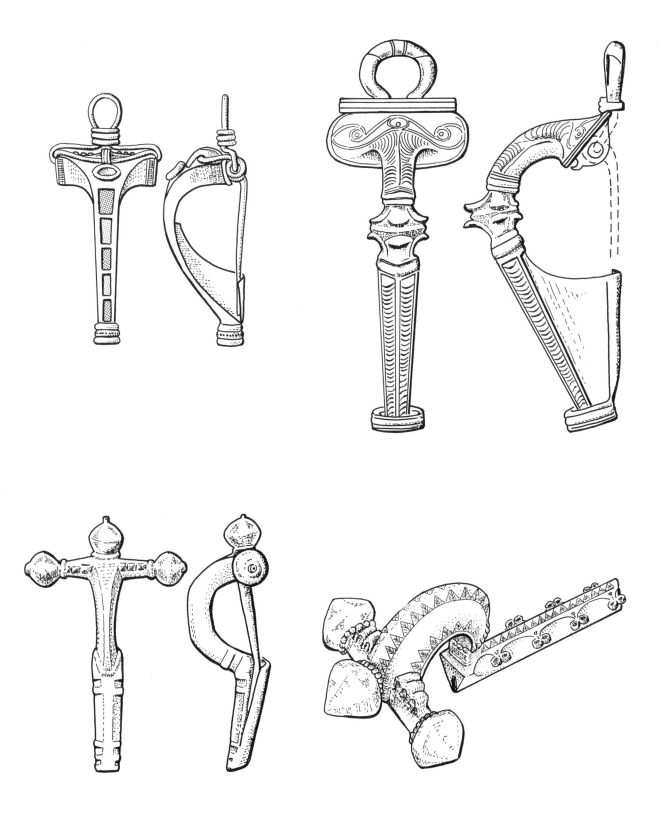

93 The bronze safety-pin brooch is, alongside pottery, the most common find from the Roman period. ABOVE LEFT The brooch of the common man and woman was small and simple. BELOW LEFT A popular variation, known as the crossbow brooch, from the late 3rd or 4th century. RIGHT Two exceptionally large brooches of gilded silver ABOVE, and gold BELOW, both enhanced with black niello.

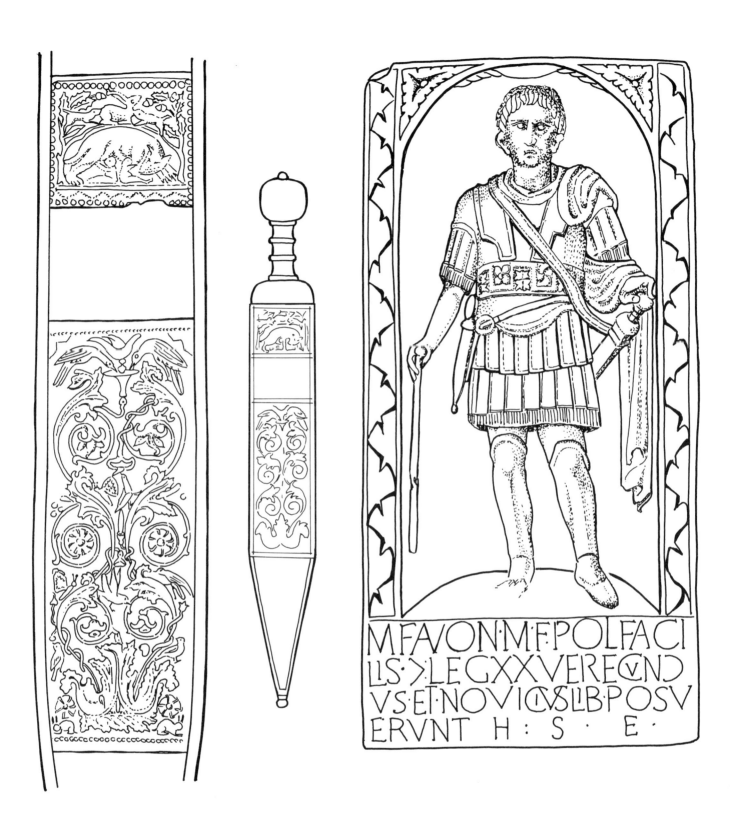

94 LEFT A reconstructed sword from the River Thames and the design on the scabbard. RIGHT A Roman centurion commemorated on a tombstone from Colchester, Essex. The inscription reads: M[arcus] FAVON[ius] M[arci] F[ilius] [son of Marcus] POL [of the Pollian tribe in North Italy] FACILIS [a horizontal V is a mark of a centurion] LEG XX [20th legion] VERECUNDUS ET NOVICIUS LIB [they were freed men] POSUERUNT [erected i.e. the stone] HSE [*Hic situs est* – Here he lies]. AD 43–60.

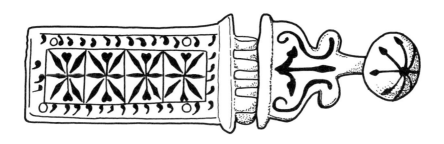

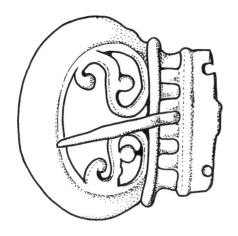

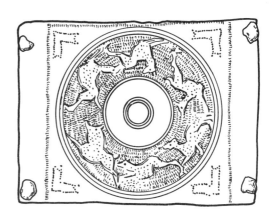

95 The centurion M. Favonius Facilis (**94**) wore a belt which was part of the standard equipment of the Roman army in the first century AD. It was of leather and covered with rectangular bronze mounts, for protection as well as decoration. Designs are in repoussé, or punched and picked out in black niello, often against a tin-plated background.

96 ABOVE An exceptionally successful design on an Italian clay lamp. It shows a chariot race in the Circus Maximus, Rome. Round the outside, top left, are the spectators and, top right, the *carceres* or starting gates, while the *spina*, the elaborate barrier round which the chariots raced, is at the bottom. Four racing chariot teams are in the centre. In a corner two gladiators fight. Actual size. BELOW Another Italian clay lamp is decorated with a gladiator fight.

97 An elaborate gladiator fight is illustrated on a Castor ware pot from Colchester, AD 175. The names of the combatants are scratched above their heads, SECUNDUS, MARIO, MEMNON and VALENTINUS.

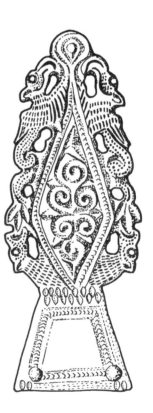

98 ABOVE LEFT The motif on this belt buckle can be identified as an Oceanus head between dolphins. On belt buckles and mounts like these, which circulated among the Germanic tribes on the borders of the Roman Empire, this motif takes on different and more fantastic forms together with the chip-carved ornament in classical spiral and scroll designs.

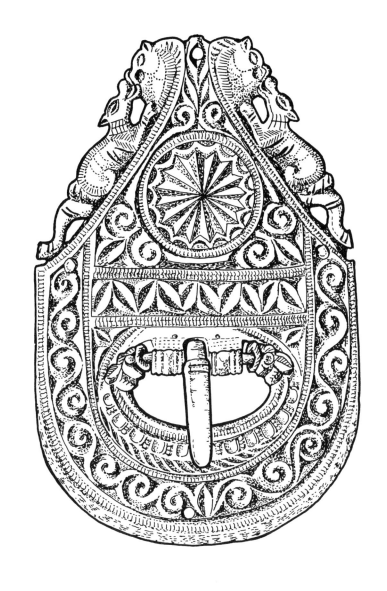

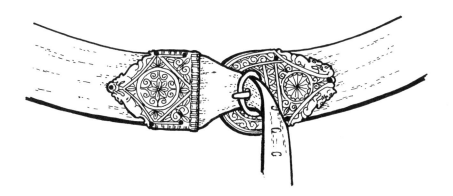

99 A reconstruction of a belt using the buckle ABOVE and plate (**98** BOTTOM LEFT) from Enns (Roman Lauriacum), Austria. Late 4th or early 5th century AD.

100 The dog was man's best friend in Roman times and he is portrayed with much sympathy in many media. Here he is in the role of guard dog, set in mosaic, at Pompeii.